Until We Meet Again

God's Eternal Plan
For His Animals

By

Asevimoru

Montford Regis, Inc.
New York

Until We Meet Again

God's Eternal Plan For His Animals
By

Asevimoru

Published by:	Montford Regis, Inc , New York
Copyrights:	May '96, Jan '04 LOC, Wash., DC
First Printing:	June 1996
Second Printing:	March 2004
Manufacturing	ArcoType Graphics, Inc.
Copy Editing:	Marvin Illman
Cover Art.	Sevi Regis
Wholesale:	Diadem Books - Direct
Catalog.	RAM Network Communications
Distribution:	James I. Wilson
Publicity:	Ascending Arts
Production Rights:	The Regis Movie Media Company, Inc.
Website:	www.montfordregis.com

Prayer Of Dedication

I dedicate this Book
To Almighty God, Father of all the living,
Whose merciful hand tenderly caresses
Every one of His beloved creatures;
And Whose eyes overflow with love,
Justice, wisdom, and compassion.
And
To all of the people who love and care for
One another and for His precious animals,
That their selfless labors
Be rewarded in this life and in the next,
So that their hearts are made glad.
And
To all of the animals themselves,
Who give so much in so many ways,
Often to those who scarcely appreciate it.
For they have suffered much
And continue to endure hardship
At the hands of those
Who were called to love and care for them.
For all that they have taught us
For all the love and nourishment
They provide for us
For all the beauty and vitality they exude,
Let them all be blessed forever
On Earth and in Heaven.
Amen.

Until We Meet Again

"... Truly I say to you,
to the extent that you did good
to one of the least of these,
you did good unto Me."
(Matthew 25:45b)

It had been one of the most wonderful days we shared during our four years together: a day of unrestrained freedom and unfurling adventure.

On Saturday, May 10, fleas, ticks, worms, parasites, and spoiled food encountered in the grass were no longer a cause for concern. He could run freely through meadow after meadow exploring, investigating, and rejoicing while I watched like a proud parent. There it was, a little glimpse of heaven set aside just for us and we eagerly ran out to greet it together.

At 6:30 in the evening the golden sun was still high in the sky as I walked Cherry across the green to the veterinarian's office. He had a brain tumor that was not safely operable. Thus the doctor would have to decide the best course of treatment for him based upon a reasonable prognosis.

Uncle Jim stood beside Cherry while the verdict was read. Across the way, I prayed under a leafy maple tree in the park we had just played in. I was asking the Lord to extend his life if it was possible and to send Cherry back to me on the road to recovery.

1

A few minutes before 7:00, I saw the sun shift from its radiant position, where it had appeared immovable all day like a painting set onto a cobalt blue canvas. But then right on the hour, it began its descent into night. And at that moment, I knew that he was gone. The vet had put my friend to rest.

Cherry first came to me one hot midnight in July while I was driving back to Brooklyn in the right lane of the Belt Parkway, a few miles west of Kennedy Airport. I had just called home to say that my trip to Connecticut went well and that I was only about twenty minutes away.

As soon as I clicked off my cell phone, a car about a quarter mile ahead of me, skidded onto the littered dirt shoulder and stopped briefly along the highway. Then I saw someone dump something out of the passenger side, shut the door, and speed off.

I slowed down not knowing what to expect when an animal rose up from the dust and walked into the road directly into on-coming traffic, right in my lane. The animal stood there frozen in fear. On my approach, it looked like a raccoon, so I honked my horn in rapid succession trying to scare it to safety. But it didn't move. I honked again, but to no avail. As I got closer, it looked like a large long-haired, orange cat. So I slowed down to a crawl. When I was within a hundred feet of the animal, I was able to identify it and then, hopefully, I'd know what to do.

Amazed to find a pedigree Pomeranian dog thrown essentially to his death, I stopped the car and got out to rescue him. Though I was afraid that the dog might bite me out of fear, I gently approached him to establish a rapport. Seeing that he was so shaken that he was unlikely to attack me, I quickly picked him up and carried him into my car.

But this was a mutually dangerous operation because a violent, road-raged man had pulled up and gotten out of his car to menace me. At the same time, other motorists were honking and shouting profanities out of their windows because I stopped in the right lane on a blind curve in order to shield the dog. The crazed man was scaring the animal, so while I tried to keep either of them from attacking me I had to also prevent the dog from bolting into the middle lane out of fear.

Once we were securely back in my car, the dog stood up for about one minute and then calmly took his seat beside me, a place he faithfully upheld until his death.

The bond between us formed in an instant, it was destiny and we both knew it. Although because this was my first dog, I was concerned if I'd know how to properly handle his needs once we got back home. I already had four cats in the house, so I wasn't sure how this was going to work out for the long haul. But there was a thrill having him by my side. He was so calm and secure despite the fact that moments earlier he was terrified and almost run over.

The week before I had said a little prayer: simply, *"Lord, now that we've gone into contract to buy a house, and we don't have to worry about landlords anymore, maybe I'll finally be able to have a dog."* Seven days later, he was received. But I needed his name, so while we rode along, I prayed again. *"Lord, tell me his name."* Asking several times and struggling with some ideas of my own, I finally heard that sweet, quiet voice say to me, *"'Cherry'."* *"His name is Cherry."*

'Cherry?' I thought! Why that? I asked. Then it clicked in my understanding, because he is small and red, because he will bring cheer wherever he goes, and because he will be Mon Cheri. And all of these proved to be true because everywhere we went children flocked to Cherry and loved playing with him. He was so extraordinarily beautiful that people would yell out of passing cars to compliment him. One summer afternoon while walking together in Southampton, two elegant women paused in their promenade to admire him then they turned to me and said, *"He's royalty, this dog. He's a prince isn't he?"* Of course, I agreed.

They were not the only ones to call him a prince, and so poignant is it that he came to me in rags. Under his filthy, matted fur coat was a skinny malnourished body suffering from parasites. So the very next day of our meeting, he went to the vet and the groomer to become the dog he was meant to be and put on his royal robes.

Since it was still summer, he was given a "lion cut" where the mane and the tail are left fluffy and the body fur is shaved off. He was so cute like this that on the way home, a little boy grabbed his mother's arm yelling, *"Mommy, look, a baby lion."*

Eventually, with much exercise and lots of home cooking he went up to eight pounds of solid, tugging muscle. Since Pomeranians are descendents from Icelandic sledding dogs and from the German Spitz, they are fairly strong at pulling weight for their humble size and they like to lead the way. He also became aggressive about taking on the day, after all he was an unfixed male, and had a lot of adventure on his mind.

Only another animal lover would understand what I mean when I say we were dogs together. Since he couldn't really come into my world, though he surely tried, I was able to enter into his. By doing this our relationship strengthened and our communication deepened.

I took him everywhere; he became my son. We were, tossed out of outdoor cafes, supermarkets, parks, beaches, arboretums, and many other places which limited my recreational activities a great deal. But whenever I had the chance I would sneak him into another place and give him an experience that made our time together wonderful. It became a game after a while to see how much we could get away with before we got caught. If only we had met in Paris, we could have savored all of these excursions without being spoken to and treated like "dogs."

One of the funniest things Cherry ever did was the day he jumped into the driver's seat and put his paws up on the steering wheel trying to turn it. He loved to ride in the car while I hugged him most of the time.

But there were some difficult moments too. A couple of times, including the first night that I brought him home, he had become suddenly ill and needed immediate intervention. And later when the tumor began to affect his personality, my darling lover boy nipped on a few occasions. But I didn't come down too hard on Cherry because I knew he'd been abused through most of the nine years or so he lived before finding his way to one who'd love him.

How beautiful he was that last day, skipping over little hills, running through the lush fields, his mane blowing in the gentle breeze while he wore his broadest smile. I remembered how he was in the freshly fallen snow when he'd leap over drifts like a deer, and in the summer when he'd splash around in the little white tub we also used to bathe him.

All of these moments passed by my heart as I sat under the tree knowing they'd come to an end. It was then that a miracle took place. While I was looking up at the sky, I saw Cherry ascending into heaven. Someone was holding him under his arms the same way I used to lift him, and he was held so as to face me with his tiny back feet dangling down.

As he was rising I watched every nuance of his facial expressions. At first he was looking down toward me wearing his big smile, with the tip of his tongue curling out, and a sparkle of appreciation in his eyes. He looked tired but contented and I saw that he thanked me in his heart for all that I'd done for him. And the tiredness I saw was from the full life that I had given him on top of the many years of suffering that preceded it.

At first there was no sense of death, it was more like he was simply being transported from a bound state to a free one. But then the most amazing thing happened. As he passed up through a high horizon, his eyes shifted from looking down at me on earth to looking up into heaven. This is the moment that confirmed the reality of this vision to me because I could never have imagined this in my own thinking.

As soon as his eyes shifted to look into the pastures of heaven his expression changed. Instantly he was beaming with joy and filled with luminosity that poured back out of his eyes. His playful smile broadened to express an ecstasy beyond what I'd ever known or observed. Cherry became so thrilled and excited at what he was seeing that I myself got caught up in the moment. He knew where he had come from and was visibly amazed at where he was going to. The overwhelming happiness that I saw in his face was indescribable. The next moment, he slipped out of sight until the day when we meet again along the great celestial Iditarod.

In his treasured memory, I offer up this prayer:

Thank You, Almighty God,
Father of all creation, Keeper of life,
For answering my prayer for a dog.
Thank You that the one You gave me
Was more perfect and compatible
Than any I could have chosen for myself.
Thank you for the precious time we shared
And for the memories we made together.
Thank You for the lives we touched
And all the love we carried into the world.
Thank You for what we taught one another
And for the wisdom we exchanged.
Thank You for accepting Cherry
Into Your glorious kingdom
Where he now freely enjoys Your glory
And can never suffer again.
And thank You, also, Lord Jesus Christ,
For teaching and enabling us to love the loveless
And to help the helpless as shown by Your example.
Thank You for esteeming all who've been discarded
and for exalting those who've been unjustly abased.
Thank You for every new beginning
And every fulfilled end, that You provide
For those who love and trust in You.
And thank you for the lasting beauty
That You write into every story
And faithfully extract from every good life.
Amen.

I've often heard people say that the reason they don't adopt a pet is that it will make them too sad when it dies. Unfortunately this point of view discounts all of the pleasurable time shared along the way to that inevitable day, and also disregards the urgent need that many animals have right now for adoption into households where they can bestow their unconditional love.

Surely it is true that as wonderful as life can be, every living creature is under a death sentence that will eventually be carried out. And for this, there is no court of appeals. Though some people behave as if they're going to escape death somehow, the fact is that none of us will. Death is an absolute finality, and with complete impartiality, it is the great equalizer for man and beast alike.

The Scripture reads, "For the fate of the sons of men and the fate of beasts is the same. As one dies so does the other; indeed, they all have the same breath and there is no advantage for man over beast for all is vanity. All go to the same place. All came from the dust and all return to the dust. Who knows that the breath of man ascends upward and the breath of the beast descends downward to the earth?" (Ecclesiastes 3:19-21)

King Solomon spoke to the issue of animal redemption in these verses which also contain other insights. But here is proof that it has long been debated whether or not creatures other than humans have any afterlife apportioned to them, or if they too have immortal souls that are accountable to God.

9

The topic of this debate is the reason for the writing of this Book, because I not only believe, but intend to logically prove, that Solomon's supposition contains the answer: that animals do live forever and that God, the Creator of all things and living beings, has an eternal plan for them.

It is evident that we will all have to surrender our bodies some day. No matter how much we take care of our physical selves and try to slow down the aging process, we live in a world where material decay is inherent and omnipresent. As a result, we will also have to endure the sorrow of losing those we know and love. But understand this, every living creature who possesses the breath of life, also has an eternal soul, whose final depository is not the grave, but rather the afterlife.

Since we know that we must leave this world at some unknown moment, it is imperative that we consider two critical things while we yet live. We must choose where we want to spend our forever, because the eternal soul within us will never cease to exist, but rather will journey on to its rightful place of which there are only two options. We must also consider the legacy that we have left behind in this world; for these are the two ways by which we are immortalized.

Most will agree that the world sighs in relief when the wicked perish, but groans in sorrow when the righteous come to their end. Even if a person's sphere of influence is shallow, his deeds will still resonate and impart a lasting impression.

Contrary to the beliefs of some, you cannot alter a person's fate after he has died. You cannot wish or pray him out of his evil ways or circumvent his just desserts in the past tense. When a person or an animal perishes, his beliefs, his deeds, and his memory are concretely set in stone, solidified by the individual's free will having been exercised through the duration of his entire life.

Though our spiritual redemption is primarily based upon the integrity and truthfulness of what we believe, our eternal reward is predicated upon the deeds that we perform on Earth, as well as whatever we entertain in our hearts and minds whether hidden or manifest. It is human nature to want to write one's own terms and agreements on important matters, especially one as monumental as this. However, we must understand that these statutes and stipulations were constructed long before we came around with our valises full of opinions and objections.

The last comment that I will make regarding the salvation of the human soul in this Book is this: if we choose to be with Christ and live our days for and with Him, then we shall be entitled to join Him when we finish our labors in this life. But if we live in unbelief upholding ourselves as mini-gods, or live selfishly with only our own concerns in our hearts, or practice wickedness without conscience, then we will most assuredly be sent away from God and His paradise on the day of judgment. And this is both just and certain.

11

The immense suffering that Christ willingly endured for our sake is a firm testament to the fact that sin is no laughing matter; rather it is capable of forever separating us from those whom we love. In the secret place of all of our hearts, we know it, yet we still find ways to deny it. Some go to psychics or channelers who pretend to commune with deceased loved ones, but they are as skilled in their deceptions as are magicians. This practice is deemed a sin and it is referred to as necromancy, and at one time, the law declared it punishable by death.

I know this is a difficult teaching to receive, though we are fortunate to live under the Messianic covenant of grace, a grace that we too often take for granted. For this reason, the path of redemption has been laid down for you; for if you learned all about the ways that animals are received into heaven, but in living lost your own way, then you may tragically not make it up to that glorious reunion in paradise to again see those whom you love.

Therefore, let God's blessings be upon all of my compassionate animal-loving readers as I take this moment to present to you, the Good Shepherd, Jesus Christ, Who said, *"I am the Good Shepherd who lays down His life for His sheep."*(John 10:11) The Lord also explains that He has sheep from many pastures, meaning that His salvation is available for all the peoples of the world, but only if they walk through the "sheep gate." And He is that gate. *"Jesus therefore said to them again, "Truly, truly I say to you, I am the door of the sheep.""* (John 10:7)

12

One of the activities that a follower of Christ is called to is to shepherd both humans and animals who are in physical and spiritual need.

Ashley was one of my sheep, but because of certain behaviors that she expressed, and acts that she committed, I genuinely worried about "Chikki" on the day that she died knowing that God cares about the thoughts and deeds of both human and animal persons.

When she was first placed into my hand, she was only the size of a mouse. A man ran up to my car in the rain while I was filling up at a local gas station. He handed me a small, yellow plastic box and pleaded with me to take the kitten he'd rescued from a car's exhaust system. Before I could say a word or even open the lid to see what was inside, he jumped back into his car and took off.

Then she squeaked, so I opened the cover to peak in and I saw gigantic gray marbles, eyes full of adventure that eventually turned bright emerald like the flourish of nature that she so loved. Her tiny body was still moist and covered with soft stripes in shades of gray, occasional white plumage, and a beige belly with black spots like a baby wild cat. The fluffy white cheeks, extra-long whiskers, and matching gloved paws made her truly irresistible.

At the time I had two elderly cats that were like an old, married couple who were in no urgent need of being chased around the house by a spunky toddling troublemaker. But what choice did I have? I was hooked at first glance as the most amazing aspect of "the Chik" was what happened in the first moment of our mutual gaze, in the twinkling of an eye.

When I opened the box to look inside, her salmon-colored nose was right up at the top sniffing around and trying to poke through. Just then, like in a Looney Tunes cartoon, a string of juicy, red hearts came pouring out of her huge eyes like they were about to be strung around my neck. Each of the hearts was perfectly formed and sweet like a candy Valentine. And I knew that they were the contents of her heart overflowing out toward me like a river. How could I refuse?

So I went home with another cat, though she was different from all the rest with her comedic antics and feisty temperament. And attempting to eat banana, cantaloupe, potato, and avocado around her was decidedly dangerous. Ironically she hated chicken, though we called her "Chikki;" instead she loved fruit, especially after a rigorous afternoon of tree climbing, branch leaping, and vine swinging like a chimp. I eventually found out from a breeder that Ashley was half Abyssinian, which accounted for some of her unusual personality traits, fine bones, and slender muscularity.

At first my two elder cats were overwhelmed by Ashley's playfulness. To be fair to them, I had only two choices: either to find another home for Ashley or to bring home another kitten that could keep up with her. Enter, Tiffany.

Tiffy was a terrified half seal-point Siamese kitten about the same size and age of Ashley, and a similar breed to my older cats. She had been left at a local shelter for adoption. Tiffany was so timid that she'd back-peddle into a tight, little ball whenever someone would try to reach for her. After I brought her home, she remained out of sight for three days before emerging to investigate her new home and meet her new family.

Even though Tiffy was afraid of people, she took to other cats very well. Since the two older cats were also part Siamese, (seal-point, natural mink Tonkinese, which are a cross between Burmese and Siamese), Tiffany found it very easy to snuggle up with them as they rested. Soon Ashley followed. But the funniest thing is that meek and mild Tiffany was the one who chased Ashley from pillar to post around the house. Fortunately the two kittens kept each other occupied leaving Tuskany and Cylkie to snuggle securely without being repeatedly pounced on. The plan worked.

This was a very happy time with the four cats. Since Cylkie had been spayed from her youth she was never able to have her own kittens. But she was so motherly and affectionate that she deserved to know the joy of raising young. She quickly took to the task and taught them whatever they needed to know. And the sweetest sight was seeing the four of them curled up into a hot, purring swirl on my bed.

But the two little girls had their jobs to do, and that's why they were brought into my life. My job was to care for them and their job was to extend my life and give me the fire power I needed to make a succession of difficult, major changes.

At that time I was very ill with undiagnosed Type I Diabetes which I was apparently born with. The chronic disease had caused a variety of severe side effects, some of which were life threatening. For some reason, no doctor found the root of my problems. They tested for everything but that and whatever they found, they never connected the dots.

Ashley was a great warrior; she would face anything and win without the least concern over the possibility of defeat. Not only did I watch this trait grow in her daily, as she'd snatch fly after fly from the air, but I also cultivated it in her using athletic challenges. She was naturally sporty and loved to play handball off the wall. We'd use an aluminum foil ball and I'd toss it to her. She would then bang it off the wall one, two, three, even four times before hitting it back to me.

By far the funniest but also most inexplicable feat she had ever performed happened one relaxed afternoon when she found an opportunity to wage war on Jiffy-Tiffy at an unsuspecting moment. The Chikk was sitting with her belly down on a desk in the living room as the Tiffster passed by the dining room. As soon as her target was sited, she lifted straight up into the air, as though she levitated, and without catapulting herself using her legs, they were still tucked beneath like retracted landing gear, she flew straight across the room, without dipping, like a heat-seeking missile. This defied all of the laws of nature, science, gravity, and logic. I'm laughing as I write this, because it was hilarious. Truly, words cannot describe it justly.

When the owners of the house we rented sold the property, we were suddenly faced with having to vacate without any place to go. Since most of the apartments we tried to rent would not accept the cats, we had only two choices once again: either put the cats up for adoption or buy a house. Since I was chronically ill and our finances reflected it, buying a house on short notice seemed like the impossible dream. But putting the cats to sleep or giving them up was really not an acceptable option. So we persevered and with God's help and Ashley's driving force, we overcame all of those obstacles and succeeded in buying a house.

Not long after we moved, Tuskany became ill and died. He was almost nineteen and the stress of moving affected him. Dogs move around easily because they bond directly to their masters, but cats also attach to their premises and it is more difficult for them to adjust to sudden change. So Cylkie, having grown up as a baby beside Tuskany, was now a widow.

To ease her pain, I bought a carved wooden version of Tuskany, who we also called "Biggie," in a store and placed it beside her favorite nesting spot. Though she showed me with a wink and a smile that she understood my intentions, the statue just didn't fill the void. So I went back to the shelter in search of a young male cat.

Truthfully, I would have done anything for Cylkie because through all the years I'd had her, she was my faithful nurse and companion. I never had to persuade her to join me for some quality time or a healing cat nap. And whatever part of my body hurt at the moment, she knew and would sit right on it to serve as a vibrating hot water bottle. Our souls were very close as we shared one breath.

She was "the runt of the litter," the breeder said. He kept hiding her behind his other hearty felines saying that she was sick and too small to be of any value. But that beautiful, little milk chocolate angel was exactly the one who appealed to me most. She needed me, so I took her right away.

Biggie was a year older and quite delighted when she came into his life. Since they were cousins from the same breeder, they bonded immediately. I can honestly say that one of the most charming love stories I have ever watched was the one between these two cats. I know there are many others, but I was privileged to live among that one.

It's amazing how much love animals exude into the atmosphere when they are kept cozy and properly cared for. Tuskany and Cylkie sent up sweet puffs of love all day every day and it would fill the house with perfume transforming it into a fragrant garden. I could always rely on its presence. So when Cylkie's hour of need came, I wanted to be there to meet it.

The shelter didn't have too many young cats that day. They had mostly older females that might have been competitive with Cylks when what she needed then was comfort. I looked through the three main adoption kennels and found no one suitable. There was one more room that the attendant almost steered me away from because it only had two kittens in it. So I asked to go in and see them.

The first cage had a frightened Tiger Tabby kitten, a gray one with black stripes and paws. I called the attendant to verify the gender, and yes, he was male. I chose him right away. All the other cages were empty except one, which I noticed on the way out of the room. I stopped a moment to take a look when a gray kitten got right up and came over to lick my finger unceasingly. As usual, not being able to resist, I took her too.

Ginger, a Russian Blue and Burmese blend had been put up for adoption along with her brother, but someone took the male and left the female behind. She was lonely.

Tiger, the small striped male with black gloves and boots, was found in the street near the shelter and he was afraid of everything. He used to ball up in the house like a little hedgehog, until he was big enough to fend for himself.

Once again, Cylkie took them right in and mothered them to adulthood. Now she was the adoptive parent of four orphans who were fortunate to be taken in and raised as her own. She was particularly fond of Tiger and was very pleased as he grew up. However, Ashley and Tiffany weren't so happy about the newcomers and they made their displeasure known.

We can learn a lot about life and ourselves from the animals, though too often we may find that we emulate their negative behaviors, especially in competitive situations when cooperating would be a much better option to exercise. Yet in many ways, to tell some folks that they're behaving like animals would be a complement and a few steps up from the level they're actually on. In some ways, animals are much better and more decent than people are and their wild nature is much more reasonable and comprehensible than those considered civilized. Still we feel superior. But are we?

When Tiger and Ginger were about three years old, Cylkie began to fail and she died. At this time it seemed like a plague had hit my house for some unknown reason, because sadly at the same time, Ashley and Tiffany passed away very young, only about five. The three little girls were buried together.

A short time later, Tiger was struck down by a mystery illness that gradually paralyzed him. I couldn't believe what was happening and there seemed to be no explanation for it. He began first with a limp which went away for a while but then it returned with a vengeance. I thought that Ginger may have chased him around the house and that he got hurt trying to escape.

Then he squeezed under a cabinet to hide and wouldn't come out even to eat. We had to place his food and water underneath and put another shallow box nearby in order to keep him going. We couldn't capture him because he would squish away and we didn't want to further injure him.

After a time, Teager came out again. We thought that our prayers were answered and that he was alright. But suddenly he became a quadriplegic, unable to move anything except his head. Only then were we able to catch him and run to the vet, where he died that evening, still undiagnosed.

Of all the losses I've had with animals, this one was the most heart-breaking and also puzzling. Tiger was such a gentle, retiring little male cat who never did anything wrong. I can't imagine why this was on his path other than the hard fact that many of the kittens found in the street are impaired because they did not receive ample mothering and were likely exposed to damaging, harsh conditions at an age too early to tolerate. I loved Tiggy and was very sad at being completely powerless to help him. But maybe he had done his job – to comfort Cylkie and be a companion to Ginger. Who can understand these things? But we can be sure, that there are reasons for everything though we may never know them.

Ginger had, at this point, lost over seven family members – her brother, Tuskany, Cylkie, Ashley, Tiffany, Tiger, and Cherry, and she was showing signs of the trauma. So I went shopping for another male cat because she is very sociable and loves to be around her own kind.

Since all of the cats, including Ginny, loved Cherry so much, I wanted to find a cat that had the same mane but was also similar in breed and nature to her hoping that this would make for a splendid union. For about three weeks I called the shelters and cat rescue groups to see if the perfect male could be found, when one afternoon I got a call back. It was from one of the rescuers that had seen a flyer posted up in a pet shop.

When I saw his picture in the store, I knew that I had to have him. He is a magnificent gray, long-haired Russian Blue with a full regal mane, huge tufted paws, and a very gentle nature. His name is Sparrow and he bonded well with Ginger, both of whom I am now privileged to have at home.

For the blessing of knowing my cats, I offer up this prayer:

Thank You, God, for the blessing of these cats
For You, Lord Jesus, are called the lion of Judah,
And these domestic cats delicately reflect
That mysterious and regal aspect of Your nature.
Thank You for their sweetness and enthusiasm,
Their affection, peace, and self-sufficiency.
And please protect those poor cats
Who are not under loving care.
Find a safe place for every one
Receiving each one into Your compassionate hands
At the end of his/her days.
Amen.

"...And He said to them,
"Go into all the world
and preach the gospel to all creation."
(Mark 16:15)

There is already much taught and written about the eternal destiny of man. But the question of the afterlife of animals is largely unaddressed except by the wonderful attention paid them by St. Francis of Assisi. He so loved the animals that he faithfully cared for them and preached the Gospel to them. There are many stories of his devotion to the animals and his spiritual bond with them in the light of God's presence.

Therefore this book is specifically devoted to a critical examination of this issue. My purpose is to present the truth in solid Scriptural context in order to dispel the numerous false teachings circulating around on this topic. I've heard many opinions regarding this subject, but do not believe that many of the spokesmen have bothered to do their homework.

There is no question that much suffering has come upon the animal kingdom because of us. But thank God that although justice does not always appear to prevail on earth, at least it always does reign victoriously in heaven.

Unfortunately animals are useful to people in ways that are detrimental to themselves. Surely we enjoy them for companionship, but we more frequently use them for food, goods, servants for the handicapped, medical experiments, product testing, protection of property, entertainment, novelty items, and other inhumane practices.

Yet with all of our applied usages of animals we have not esteemed them worthy of possessing souls or a spiritual nature. This has been one of the tragic injustices that we have committed against the innocent and helpless fellow creatures who were created by the very same God as ourselves. We have treated them as profit-yielding commodities, rather than living and loving creatures.

Daily, various species of animals are made to suffer enormously at the hands of man. Stories of mistreatment in shelters, abuse in dysfunctional homes, conditions in slaughter houses, practices at laboratories, and wild animals caught in traps are truly heartbreaking for those who have hearts. We really must do whatever we can to change the way we treat animals and to create and enforce laws that will protect them from all manner of harm.

It is truly unfortunate that several prominent animal rights groups have exercised behaviors that are counter-productive to and reflect badly on the mission that they represent; because these advocacy groups are so needed to provide representation and defense for those who cannot offer it for themselves.

Nature is harsh enough on the animals; they do not need the added burden of what we put them through. And the Scripture makes it clear that God loves His animal kingdom and that He is displeased with our treatment of them.

Some heavy-handed interpreters of the Bible claim that the sovereignty we were granted over the animals means that we can do whatever we please with them because they were provided specifically for our usage and that they have no souls. This is a heartless and soulless misinterpretation of the holy written Word rendered by those with a chauvinistic frame of mind. Often in these same people are found gross concealed sins that have led to the distortion of God's nature as He expressed it to us in creation.

I knew one such man who was a stalwart at Church. Everyone turned to him for advice and Scriptural clarification and he was quick to provide. He was one of those *"Animals have no souls; they're only around for our convenience."* type of guys. Some years after he passed away, his daughter came forward confessing how her father sexually abused her during childhood. He had even continued his perverse gestures toward her into adulthood.

But what does God say? *"A righteous man is kind to (his) animals."* In fact, the way a person treats animals speaks volumes about his character overall, and it can be an accurate predictor of one's future behavior patterns, such as in the horrid case of sociopaths and killers who began their criminal lives by treating animals cruelly.

Any parent that willfully permits his child to mistreat other living creatures may very well be responsible for unleashing a sociopathic person into society, and he should be held accountable. Any time these behaviors emerge, they should not be taken lightly. It is not normal, it's not cute or funny; simply it is not acceptable and it must be corrected.

We clearly learn from the example of Jesus that the greater person bows to and serves the lesser; not that the greater oppresses and belittles the lesser. When someone mistreats anyone, animal or human, who is more helpless than himself, he is exercising the dark side of his nature and this should be dealt with right away or it will increase and spread into other areas of the person's life.

But again, when we are seeking an accurate understanding of God's Word, we must look for the character of Christ, the Good Shepherd, Who lays down His life for the sheep, and leaves the ninety-nine who are safely pastured to rescue the one that got lost or has strayed into harm's way.

Animals not only have amazingly similar DNA to human beings, but they also have a triune nature, composed of body, soul, and spirit. And although theirs is different from ours in some ways, it is the same in other ways.

And yes, animals do have an afterlife as do we. They either enter the kingdom of heaven or they are sent away from God, in the same way we are. The only difference is in the methods that the

Almighty Creator uses to judge and communicate with humans and animals.

People were given specific laws to obey and so too were animals given their appropriate laws, and all are subject to the same natural laws. As animals are largely unaware of our laws, we are likewise unaware of theirs, except those we refer to as instincts, behaviors that are actually expressions of the laws that God placed within them.

There are several windows in Scripture that provide insight into the laws and codes given to animals. These laws appear to be firmly established without containing any form of formal repentance or ritual atonement. Nevertheless, the animals are judged on both of the same criteria that apply to us: by their faith and their deeds.

The difference is that animals are more "programmed" than humans are, and this innate adherence to specific behaviors is called, natural instinct. They tend to respond more out of physical urges than higher thought, though they are capable of both, but the latter to a more limited degree. Although many animals have evidenced remarkable levels of intelligence, empathy, love, compassion, sensory acuity, forethought, and heroic action which all require mental ability beyond what many expect from them, animals are still grossly underestimated.

Animals do also have free will, because it is by the exercise of their wills that their deeds are evaluated and judged by both man and also by God.

Since animals will be held accountable for their actions as individuals, it is important that we recognize their spiritual nature when we deal with them. The kind treatment of our fellow creatures must include guidance toward proper behavior, and respectful care that, as is the same for our children, provides an environment in which the animal can freely grow and obey that which God has instilled within him. We must not abuse, neglect, or mistreat them in any way because this may cause them to sin.

It is true that animals, like humans, will inevitably transgress even without any provocation or assistance from the peanut gallery. Even so our responsibility to them mandates that we behave kindly, responsibly, and respectfully toward them, and that we correct their inappropriate behaviors, in some cases, by erecting obstacles to keep them from sinning. We must also pray for them and pray over them always committing them to the Lord who loves and cares for them.

The reason that Biblical information about animals is so scanty, mysterious, and metaphoric, is because God authored the Book for our consumption. There are other reasons as well such as the Biblical order of sovereignty which explains that men were given first place by God, because they are created in the direct image and likeness of Himself; whereas, women were not created directly but indirectly through Adam as is confirmed by our chromosomal blueprints. (A normal man generally has an XY pattern whereas women have XX showing that you can derive woman from man through normal replication but not vice versa.)

Scripture is replete with discussions about the acts of men, though there are only a few women of note ever discussed in detail throughout all the books of the Bible. Even the Blessed Virgin Mary, who was so honored to become the earthly mother of Jesus, is scarcely mentioned.

Over the centuries, many women have found this fact to be offensive or an indication that God views them in a derogatory or condescended light. But that is not true at all. Remember in Eden when original sin entered the world, it is written that Eve was deceived, but Adam sinned. The extra visibility given to men brings with it an additional burden and a great deal more responsibility in certain matters.

There is great significance to the order of creation during which the woman was the final character. The one thing missing from the perfect garden was an equal helpmate, a bride for God's first human son. Together, they were supposed to tend the Lord's magnificent garden and to love and care for his beloved creation, including the animals.

With this understanding, Adam was given a position of responsibility over his beloved Eve and he was also given sovereignty over everything that God made on earth. This was the inheritance he was to share with his mate.

The hierarchy of creation as expressed in the Bible is such that the highest ranking person, who is God, is spoken of most often and is preeminent in every writing as both the primary focus and as the divine Author.

The lowest level of this hierarchy, basically the plant life, is spoken of the least. We know almost nothing about God's eternal plan for his green creation, other than that God is a master conservationist and that He loves His trees, flowers, and vines more than we do. The Scripture explains that, *"The trees of the fields will clap their hands."* And that Jesus cursed the fig tree that did not produce fruit for his passing by.

This verse has a triple-application because it also refers to certain ancient Israelites who did not recognize and receive the long-awaited Messiah as He came their way, as well as to anyone, including Christians, who claim to possess faith and belong to the Lord yet do not produce the fruit of the Spirit.

However the hierarchical design of creation does explain why the truths about the afterlife of animals are concealed within the sovereign order of mankind, and can only be found by those who love the animals enough to diligently seek these mysteries out, as it is written, *"Seek Me with all of your heart, and I will show you great and unsearchable things that no man can know or find."*

Even though we have been granted authority over the animal kingdom, much the way parents have dominion over their children, God has absolute dominion over the souls and eternal destinies of all living beings. Though the body of the creature perishes, whether by natural means or resulting from maltreatment, the soul and spirit of the animal are properties belonging to God with which He will deal justly and without a single oversight.

Let us examine a few Scriptures that provide understanding about the methods of evaluation that God uses to judge individual animals with regard to their ultimate standing with Him.

The earliest account of this process is found in Genesis Chapter 6 verses 5-8, *"Then the Lord saw that the wickedness of man was great on earth, and that every intent of the thoughts of his heart was only evil continually. And the Lord was sorry that He had made man on the earth, and He was grieved in His heart. And the Lord said, "I will blot out man whom I have created from the face of the land, from man to animals to creeping things and to birds of the sky, for I am sorry that I have made them." But Noah found favor in the eyes of the Lord.""*

Until this point in history, it is stated that man and animals were both vegetarians. So their violent actions were not even attributable to hunting for survival. This passage clearly shows that man was the created being that primarily displeased God, and that although animals had also sinned and were corrupted by the dark spiritual forces of Noah's time, they were essentially destroyed in the great flood because of the sins of man.

The principle is this: when a leader is corrupt his peoples suffer because of him. We know from history that wicked kings have wrought much havoc on their peoples, as do political leaders of today that do not rule in righteousness.

When a stable full of horses burns to the ground, it is not because the horses had snarled too frequently or had failed to rise at the crack of dawn. It is because of punishment brought about by the sins of man, regardless of the hand through whom it was enacted. Sometimes these tragic occurrences are deliberately brought about by malevolent or ruthless people; other times they may happen as a result of oversight or negligence. Yet even if something like this is brought about by an "act of God," the root cause is generally of human origin, though it may be difficult to discern.

But these are some of the events that destroy the mortal body, something which is inevitable in all living things due to the process of death which entered the world by way of sin in Eden. What destroys the soul and spiritual inheritance of a living being is to continue on in sin and not return to God.

The sins of this world bring such terrible penalties down upon all the living because as they once did, they continue to open the gates for darkness to enter in as well as to force the hand of God in judgment.

Often you hear people complain that their behaviors, though they may be socially destructive, should not be challenged because individuals should be free to do whatever they want whenever they want. One example of this is abortion. The mother claims it is only her needs and wants that matter.

Whereas the baby's right to his life has no value or right of defense. Some even debate the humanity of the fetus altogether. However this deplorable act is rationalized, the killing of unborn children is a monstrous sin and tantamount to the ancient pagan practice of child sacrifice which was done to please carved idols that were imputed to be gods.

Now God harshly judged all of the lands that practiced child sacrifice and other blood shedding acts. But tragically, when the penalty falls, even the good and the innocent may suffer along with the wicked, as it is written, *"The rain falls upon the righteous as well as the unrighteous."* How sad it is when it falls upon the animals when man has brought it about. Where then is God's justice, mercy, and compassion? Let's read on.

About nine years ago I lived near a park that was home to many beautiful trees and an extended family of squirrels. Everyone loved to go there and feed them, especially the children. On occasion, an irresponsible dog owner would unleash an aggressive canine among the crowd to terrorize moms wheeling strollers and other inhabitants until a passing ranger would enforce the City leash law.

One year we had fed the squirrels so well that it produced an effervescent bumper crop of the playful little critters. This was a really fun summer that turned into an even more fun harvest season. By October, the park's pets had flourished so much that they were attracting peanut-tossing spectators of all sizes, shapes, and colors who cooed at the squirrels in almost every language.

The squirrels were very industrious and I've learned a lot about investing and asset management from them. The cutest thing about them is how they behave together sometimes, such as in the park.

What delighted the visitors so much was how they built cooperatives into old, worn limbs and performed a variety of antics there. One of the apartment complexes was near the road. This one was the most densely populated. There were at least a dozen rooms housing over ten families in that dry, curved tree.

In one window was a chubby elder squirrel hanging out waiting for some food to happen by; from another window a baby would jump out to hang upside-down, and in yet another window, perfectly posed, would be an entire family snapshot of mama, papa, and babies snuggling up together, waiting eagerly for some crunchy treats to be delivered to their address. Occasionally, in another window you might see a playful skirmish rumbling about. Truly, it was show time all the time.

We remained faithful in our feeding of them throughout the winter until the nor'easter came. It was a bad prediction: heavy snowfalls and severe north easterly winds with bitter cold temperatures. A mean winter storm was coming and we went out shopping for supplies. No time to think about the condos or anything else but personal survival, all because you never really know how these things are going to go. It's always best to plan for the worst and hope for the best.

The storm began with a circular wind pattern and sprinkling of flurries but it quickly grew in intensity. It raged on with angry gusts through the night, the entire next day, into a second nightfall. That morning we spent four hours shoveling and cleaning up the damage.

About two days passed before we thought that the squirrels might be hungry and in need of food. The snow was so heavy that it was too far to walk to the park, about a mile away, before more of the fourteen-inch accumulation was cleared.

When we finally got there, we saw many downed trees, broken limbs, and other windblown desolation. Concerned, we quickly walked through the high drifts toward the condo. But while approaching it, my heart sank. It was torn into pieces. I moved faster in case someone there was in trouble and needed immediate help. But it was too late. The squirrels were all killed in their houses and their bodies lied still in the wreckage.

I sat on the stump and broke down in tears. This was too much. Why these precious, innocent little animals that everyone loved so much? They were crushed, ripped apart, and totally devastated. My beautiful bumper crop was wiped completely out, and the tree that so hospitably provided for them was shredded by the hand of nature. "Sin!" I shouted. "All because of damned, stupid, sin!"

With snapped twigs all around, I found two pieces that I assembled into a cross and planted at the base of the condo. Then I said a special prayer of memorial for the joy that the squirrels brought to so many, and of remorse for the sins of humanity. After that, some of me went home, while another part was permanently lost to that moment.

The rest of the winter I remained emotionally frozen along with the frigid temperatures because I couldn't reconcile why the heavy hand of nature had come down so hard on something so delicate and guileless as the condo.

I know that God allows circumstances to bring man to both repentance and to justice, but the animals? What remorse or penalty did they need to realize? Although I recalled the verse that explains how impartial and broad sweeping these things can be. But where was fair mercy? That question would not be answered until the following spring.

It was a brilliantly sunny day in late June when I had the courage to visit the park again. I walked the entire loop before timidly venturing over to where the condo had been. The first thing I saw was the cross still sticking out of the memorial ground. Then I walked around the outer edge of the tree and looked up when I saw a miracle.

The condo was built into a dead trunk, one that had no leaves and whose branches were dry, broken, and gnarled. But now the tree was alive and it had an extension covered with leaves glistening in the sunlight. They were only growing from one branch. It was a curved branch that had grown very long in the shape of a bow. As I looked in at the leaves in amazement, the sun shone through them and created a brilliant green image. This reminded me of the passage in Revelation 4:2-3, *"Immediately I was in the Spirit; and behold, a throne was standing in heaven, and One sitting on the throne. And He who was sitting was like a jasper stone and a sardius in appearance; and there was a rainbow around the throne, like an emerald in appearance."*

At that moment, I heard the Lord speak to my heart and say, "Don't worry or cry anymore. They are not lost, they are with Me." I broke into tears, though this time with relief, and truthfully, it brings a tear to my eye even now as I recall this experience which further proves when Jesus says in Luke 12:6 that: *"Are not five sparrows sold for two cents? And yet not one of them is forgotten before God,"* He truly means it.

It's easy to be moved with compassion for the animals who suffer so much as they are exposed to natural hardships. While we are comfortable in our homes, the animals are out there in the elements facing the harshest of circumstances. Polar bears wander about while starving. Seals are continuously hunted by others who eat them. Mountain goats are caught in blizzards on slippery slopes, and many fall. Some animals get injured and struggle with chronic pain and disability, while others are stricken with illness. And most spend their lives fighting the wind, heat, snow, rain, fire, predators, and disease.

Because conditions for wild animals are so harsh, they must deal harshly with one another in the quest for survival. But this was not the original plan designed by God and established in Eden. It was not meant to be that lion would devour lamb, but that the regal lion would lay down peaceably with the gentle lamb. In fact this is God's promise for the world to come when He restores His creation to its original design and intention.

During Noah's time, God saw that His plan for creation had been corrupted by Satan and his demons to an intolerable degree. Things had turned so violent and dark that He was prompted to severe action, *"Then the Lord saw that the wickedness of man was great on the earth, and that every intent of the thoughts of his heart was only evil continually. And the Lord was sorry that He had made man on the earth, and He was grieved in His heart. And the Lord said, "I will blot out man whom I have created from the face of the land, from man to animals to creeping things and to birds of the sky; for I am sorry that I have made them." But Noah found favor in the eyes of the Lord.""* (Genesis 6:5-8)

In Genesis, after the flood, God changed the vegetarian order into a food chain of hunters hungry for meat. In part, this was established because the sacrificial system of law would be introduced later on. Another reason is that the predatory system keeps the behavior and propagation of wild animals in check physically, spiritually and environmentally through a type of natural persecution that maintains the ecological balance.

The predatory system is a humbling one that maintains order in a fallen world, and it also keeps animals more dependent upon God who must rely on Him to meet their daily needs. Because of their circumstances, animals need to pray a lot for food, shelter, and deliverance from evil much the way we do. This forced dependency keeps the creatures in a closer communion with their Creator and Savior who guides them through rivers, fields, mountains, and woods where the blessings and curses of life are waiting.

The attacking and killing of one animal by another and the existence of ferocious carnivores is troubling to me. I surely wish that this was not the case. It's so sad when a helpless animal is chomped into by a hungry one. And as much as I'd like to be a vegetarian, I cannot because I'm a Type I Diabetic who requires a high protein diet. These are the hard facts of this life. Nevertheless, I recognize that this functional design is also necessary since everything is so out of balance on every level. In the end, God will redeem and restore all of the innocent, animal and human alike. I can rest in this.

But I must admit that I would prefer that all of society would begin to depart from the eating of meat, though this would require dedicated scientific intervention. Yet it's now possible to grow sheets of meat in a laboratory by using cells from an animal, and with such perfected technology, killing for food could be rendered obsolete. In the fantasy of my mind, I could even imagine a world where animals were kept in wild but managed habitats where they too would not have to kill to eat, though they could be given their special food in faux hunting exercises that feel like the real thing and are designed to keep the animals sharp. But the danger here is that they would become so reliant on man's machine that they would likely fall away from dependency on, and relationship with, God. And it is considerably more dangerous for one to find his eternal soul in jeopardy than his temporal body, though surely we must responsibly guard both.

For this purpose a very strict law is given to both man and animals in Genesis 9:4-6, *"But you must not eat flesh with its life, that is, its blood. And surely I will require your lifeblood; from every beast I will require it. And from every man, from every man's brother, I will require the life of man. Whoever sheds man's blood, by man his blood shall be shed, for in the image of God He made man."*

Clearly we see in this passage and continuing in the following verses that God gave His covenant not only to man but also to the animals, as well as to all living creatures whether big or small.

Genesis 9:12-15, *"This is the sign of the covenant which I am making between Me and you and every living creature that is with you for all successive generations. I set My bow in the cloud, and it shall be for a sign of a covenant between me and the earth. And it shall come about, when I bring a cloud over the earth, that the bow shall be seen in the cloud. And I will remember My covenant, which is between Me and you and every living creature of all flesh; and never again shall the water become a flood to destroy all flesh. "*

Another reliable translation reads this way, *"I will demand an accounting from every animal and from every man too for the shedding of the lifeblood of his fellow man. "* How could the animals give such an accounting to God if they did not meet with Him face to face?

This is a two-fold statement that provides another example of the simultaneous applicability of Scripture to the natural and supernatural realms. The physical dimension of this law is commanding that every senseless murder be vindicated with the capital punishment of the perpetrator. The concurrent spiritual law handed down here applies to when God renders eternal judgment because of the principle spoken of in First Corinthians 6:9a, *"Or do you not know that the unrighteous shall not inherit the kingdom of God?"*

Whereas, *"But the fruit of the spirit is love, joy, peace, gentleness, patience, kindness, goodness, faithfulness, and self-control; against such things there is no law. "* (Galatians 5:22-23) It's amazing how effortlessly all of the domestic animals I've had the privilege to own have exercised and dwelt in the fruit of the Spirit. Yet I've never met such a person who produced the fruit without much painful pruning.

And God said against such behaviors there is no law to judge or condemn the creature who acts upon them. That means that these animals will be with God when they die. If the fruit of the Spirit is present, then so too is the Holy Spirit in the midst.

It was mentioned earlier that the Scripture teaches, *"A righteous man is kind to (his) animals."* And that the way people treat animals is a reliable gauge of their character. Yet a sacrificial system had been set up by God which used pure holy, unblemished, and naïve little lambs, goats, doves, etc., to be killed by a Levitical priest on the Temple's altar in order to pay for the sins of the people.

How could this be considered as kindness to animals yet be a fulfillment of righteousness? Is there a contradiction here? Of course, it was good for the people. Through this system God permitted a substitutionary form of atonement that suspended the judgments applicable to, and enforceable on, man for the dreadful sins he was committing. But how could this be kind to each innocent creature whose throat was to be cut and whose life was to be robbed for a wrong committed by someone else?

Since the Word is consistent in all ways it cannot be at odds with itself. First it is important to understand that the Temple priests were instructed to perform these atoning sacrifices in the most reverent, humane, gentle, efficient, and quick way. A holy priest had to also feel sorrow, tragedy, and remorse over the entire drama and the acts he had to commit as penalty and payment for people's sins.

42

It is important to understand the distinction between the ancient holy order imposed by God and pagan religions which do not uphold the righteous standards for animal sacrifice, do not have God's blessing of atonement associated with these acts, and therefore basically cast innocent lives at the feet of demons. As such, their sacrifices were, and are, pure cruelty and the squandering of life.

In this present age, no form of animal sacrifice is spiritually legitimate or acceptable to God, especially if performed for religious reasons. The sacrificial death of Jesus Christ, the Lamb of God who came to take away the sins of the world, replaced the ancient system. We now live under the grace He dispensed at the cross. But we should not feel that we have gotten off easy; because any sensitive true believer must continually look to the mirror of the cross to see his own sins and the horrible price that had to be paid for them. We should surely not take the tortured death of God's only begotten Son for granted and live in a cavalier, unbelieving fashion. For if we do, then the blessed atonement offered to us by faith will be nullified and unable to save us when we come up to deliver our accounting before God.

Also let us not take lightly the vision given to the prophet Daniel (7:9-14) as though it were a fairy tale or a figment of a man's imagination. *"I kept looking until thrones were set up, and the Ancient of Days took his seat; His vesture was like white snow and the hair of His head like pure wool."*

43

"His throne was ablaze with flames. Its wheels were a burning fire. A river of fire was flowing and coming out from before Him; thousands upon thousands were attending Him, and myriads upon myriads were standing before Him. The court was seated and the books were opened." (omitted· V11-12) *"I kept looking in the night visions, and behold, with the clouds of heaven one like a Son of Man was coming, and He came up to the Ancient of Days and was presented before Him. And to Him was given dominion, glory and a kingdom that all the peoples, nations, and men of every language might serve Him. His dominion is an everlasting dominion which will not pass away; and His kingdom is one which will not be destroyed."*

Indeed the court will sit and the books will be opened and all will be judged, both man and beast. Even angels will be judged and found either faithful or fallen. And there will be many phases of the ultimate judgment as the court will sit for many sessions, some of which God has revealed and some of which He has not. But in any case, these words are true and must not be discarded as opinion.

There is also another principle: it is referred to as reaping and sowing. It is written, *"Be ye not deceived for God is not mocked; that whatever a man sows that shall he also reap."*

About twenty years ago, about 3:00 in the morning, an object moved in the roadway while I was on my way home. As a bus passed, I saw that it was an animal. I raced up to rescue it and found a cat hit in the face by a car, bleeding profusely, and about to die. I wrapped her in a spare sweatshirt and brought her into the car.

It took me about an hour to race around and find an all-night vet. Finally I located one and ran in with her having only moments to live. The whole time I was driving around, this sweet creature was on my lap showing as much love and appreciation as she could. Through all of her pain, she weakly purred and glanced up at me.

The vet went to work right away but told me that she'd be in surgery over night and would have to convalesce in the hospital for about a week. He quoted the cost and asked if I'd be willing to pay close to $1,000 for her recovery. I agreed.

During that week I had to search for an adoptive home for her because the apartment I was renting did not permit pets. I found a wonderful woman and her husband who gladly consented. So I made arrangements with them and bought a year's supply of food and litter for them.

It's beautiful to see the people who express the most compassion in this life. The elder couple that took this cat in were themselves handicapped, the woman was in a wheelchair and the man could barely see. They had all to do but to care for their own troubles, yet they so eagerly reached out to give what little they had to one in greater need. Truly they were among the kindest people that I had ever met; unsung heroes whom the Lord knows and loves.

A year later I was riding my new, expensive touring bicycle around a congested area of Queens. I didn't like going into this neighborhood, but a friend of mine lived there and I went to visit him. Since this bicycle was built for performance, I was strapped into toe clips with cleated racing shoes and attached to the handlebars with special grip gloves.

On the way home, I was almost clear of the heavily trafficked area when a van ran a red light and came right at me broadside. As I jumped the curb, the truck did likewise and began chasing me down the block an inch off my back tire. Riding for my life while people were diving for cover on the pavement which I was about to be crushed into, a miracle happened.

There was no way that I could have gotten off that bicycle in time because it was a tall man's frame with a high bar between my legs, also I was clipped onto it, and there was only a one second distance between me and the pursuer. Somehow, in the twinkling of an eye, I found myself on the ground without a scrape or a scratch, but the van kept going, mangling my bicycle, dragging it three more blocks then down into a basement garage.

A few witnesses ran after the driver who turned out to be a drunk, unlicensed motorist who was so afraid of going to jail that she quickly paid for the damages done to my property. I didn't press any charges beyond that, I was just happy and amazed to be alive and uninjured.

About fifteen years later I was reading the Beatitudes, and when I arrived at the verse that says, *"Blessed are the merciful, for they shall obtain mercy."* I heard the soft voice of the Lord say, "Remember the cat? Remember the bicycle?" My spirit leaped with excitement at having this very tangible connection made for me, something I'd not seen before.

Whatever we do, the deeds we commit will come back to us in our hour of need; and whatever we send out, we will get back, whether good or evil, and it will be remembered in this life as well as in the next. And God's records are perfectly accurate.

But going back to the issue of the Temple sacrifice ordered by God, the way that kindness was offered to the sacrificial animals had to have been in the form of eternal rewards provided in exchange for the involuntary removal of its young, pure, and tender life. In the spiritual realm, this was a great honor bestowed upon these animals, and I firmly believe that we will see them all luxuriating in the great, lush green pastures of heaven.

I can state this with confidence because if the animals were pure and blameless enough to be acceptable to God as atonements for sin, then they also would need to have a spiritual purity worthy of His presence. After all, before the Lord's death the animals were serving in the priestly redemptive plan with their blood offered up as payment for the sins of man.

This is one of the many alignments of Jesus and the animals found in Scripture. Another one is the fact that the Lord was born in a stable full of animals because there was *"no room for Him at the Inn."* Imagine, there was no room available for a pregnant young woman about to give birth at night. The proprietor of the Inn must have seen her urgent need for a place of repose, yet he turned her away. The world of man had no space for the King to enter, but the humble abode of the animals gladly welcomed in the Lamb of God.

Why did God choose lambs for sacrifice? And why is His Son likened to one? Some years ago I visited a large residential farm in New England. They had all kinds of animals roaming contentedly about there. I spent the entire day watching them, feeding them, and basically getting to know them on a variety of levels. I recently found a picture of me from that day, holding the Bible open preaching the Gospel to a couple of auburn ponies.

There was one pen that was full of sheep. The chubby elders were quite pushy about who was going to have access to the feed being offered. I had to work hard to get around their strong front lines to make sure the little ones could also enjoy the feast. Then a lactating mother came out of the barn to see what was going on and her two baby lambs came with her attempting to nurse as they go. And I must admit, these young lambs were the most adorable little creatures on the farm.

More than any other animals I'd ever seen, they had a perfect purity of purpose, an unsurpassed innocence, an endearing helplessness, a gentleness, and a total obliviousness to any form of evil. Even canine pups, as innocent as they are, are aware of any evil around them, though they have not yet grown to an age where they can act against or along with evil forces. But these lambs had no knowledge, no sense, and no awakening that such even exists.

Though it is written that we must *"be wise as serpents and harmless as doves,"* the knowledge of evil can also be an evil unto itself. We must be aware of the darkness that is around us, but we are prohibited from operating by way of these forces no matter what the circumstances are. In addition to that we are told that it is a grievous sin to delve into and learn about *"the deep things of Satan."*

It is important to remember that there were two trees in the Garden of Eden. One was the Tree of Life which represents Christ, and the other was the Tree of the Knowledge of Good and Evil which represents Satan. As the time that creation was set in the Garden, Lucifer had already fallen from his lofty place and had faced off with God over the rights to both the heavenly throne and the Messianic throne of earth. Had this not happened, then the second tree may not have been temptingly there.

What that tree provided was a doorway by which Satan could come into the world and reach beyond what levels of access had been entrusted to him by God before his fall. Now man could become

Satan's agent of entry and provide the opportunities needed for the devil to go after his coveted throne. It's not only the acknowledgement of the Adversary that gives him entry but also the acceptance of the rotten, yet enticing, fruit that he offers.

It would have been enough for Adam, Eve, and every other inhabitant of the Garden to have known only good and to be entirely innocent of evil. But that's how the devil operates, he baits people with a little truth, a little promise, a little pleasure, and a little goodness, then he hooks his dark lie onto the end of it. Then before you know it you cannot escape his reeling.

Unfortunately animals are subjected to the same malevolent trickery as humans, as we recount that it was the *"crafty serpent"* who was the first one successfully tempted, who then caught and ran with the false wisdom that destroyed everything it its path. God immediately judged the serpent for his participation in the devil's scheme by casting him down to crawl around on his belly. God held him accountable because the creature was intelligent and capable of knowing better, and he was in some sort of communication with his Creator during which he rebelled against the instructions given him.

Now how could all of this have happened, one might ask? If Lucifer was created beautiful and perfect, then how did he become the hideous devil? Who tempted him? How could something flawless become the origin of every flaw? Why didn't God create everything in an incorruptible state from the beginning? How could He have allowed ruination and decay to enter the splendor of His creation and destroy it? These are all valid questions and the very same ones that I asked many years ago when I was searching for higher truth.

Yet all of these questions are answered as they converge into a single truth. In fact, they are all explained by one word: love. Now by definition, love must be chosen or it is not itself, it is not love. The Scripture says that *"God is love."* This means that God is the ultimate personification of love, that all of His ways are love, that His divine purpose is always the propagation and restoration of love, that He dwells in the substance and state of love, that He is the source of all love, and even that He is literally made of love.

However, if someone is programmed to love then he cannot actually love at all. This is because love must be a living choice and act of one's volition when other options are available. The reason for this is because of that the vitality love must have in order to be alive and agree with its definition. If someone loves out of fear, he is not loving from his heart but only professing it for survival. If someone loves out of necessity or compulsion, then he is only meeting his own needs and has not comprehended what love really is.

Love is the open-hearted recognition of the wonderful qualities possessed by the object of one's love that surpass the attributes of others and causes the giver to ascribe goodness and value to the object.

And because God's love is true, He cannot accept any imperfect or counterfeit love. The very reason that He created all things was to artfully express and splendidly replicate His love in all of His beautiful living beings.

Lucifer was created as a beautiful archangel endowed with many powers and granted extensive sovereignty. But his love was not perfect, because he became enamored with his own attributes, and out of narcissism, came to covet the throne thinking he could surpass God to rule the universe. This is the first sin and the origination of all evil. But who tempted him to think this way? Ironically it was his own blessings that tempted him because he was made on such a high level that it was easy for him to take the leap to think he could be God.

But God allowed Lucifer to be corrupted by his own thinking because it was part of His plan for creation as the devil would later serve as a magnet to draw away all those of God's earthly family who did not love Him in spirit and in truth, those whose love would be tested and found false. It is a way of purifying and distilling all of creation for the sake of gathering together His kingdom where genuine, chosen love rules, that after being tried, will remain pure forever. It can be compared to the crushing of coal into its crystalline state of gleaming diamond which can no longer be reduced.

Scripture teaches us what love is and how it is expressed: *"Love is patient, love is kind, and is" "not jealous; love does not brag and is not arrogant, does not act unbecomingly; it does not seek its own; is not provoked, does not take into account a wrong suffered, does not rejoice in unrighteousness, but rejoices with the truth; bears all things, believes all things, hopes all things, endures all things. Love never fails; but if there are gifts of prophecy, they will be done away; if there are tongues, they will cease; if there is knowledge, it will be done away. For we know in part, and we prophesy in part; but when the perfect comes, the partial will be done away with."* (1Corinthians 13:4-10)

It's wonderful how easily some animals feel and express all of the attributes of love; except in the case of baby lambs, it is certainly possible for them to do otherwise. But they don't. We should take a lesson or two from them. We have become so complicated in our thinking that we've corrupted ourselves like Lucifer, wanting to be and play God, replacing Him with images and extensions of us.

But how patient, kind, faithful and all the rest is my little Maltese companion, Jesse Merciful, who is seated at my left side at this very moment, curled up in his fleece basket? How wonderful are the pure, good, and simple things of life that money can't buy but that love alone grows and flourishes. This tiny rescued dog shows so much love, honor, obedience, and appreciation for his home that it makes me cherish him more each day. All he wants is to give me his love, devotion, and other treasures.

Jesse came from a home where he was being neglected and treated harshly. When I first saw him, my heart melted because he was beautiful, tiny, and had downcast eyes. The minute the previous owner placed him in my arms, the dog clung to me as if he had always been my own. The man who gave him to me really loved the little dog, but he worked very long hours and his teenagers were at home treating the animal roughly like he was a toy. So I asked for the doggie and he gave him to me in September. I could never put into words how adorable, pure, and sweet is the love of this magnificent, well-behaved and paper-trained, precious soul.

Little dogs are often found in bad situations because people buy them thinking they are stuffed toys to play with, but when the owners find out that the animals have real daily needs that must be met like grooming, playing, loving, learning, physical functions, health, walking, companionship, mental stimulation, and integration into their families' lives, they may discard the dogs in shelters to shed the responsibility altogether or treat them badly out of resentment for the demands made over their care.

In either case, little dogs are in peril, yet the love that they give is among the most pure on earth. Pet owners need to understand that little dogs have little bladders and that they need to urinate more frequently. And that breeds with long hair require more frequent and gentle grooming. They are also very sensitive to the cold because they are close to the ground, and their bones are delicate requiring a special handling. I've seen people try to pick up small dogs by their front legs as though they were lifting a chair up by its spindles. This is not only a painful way to lift an animal but it could break their legs or dislocate them. If only we'd operate by the golden rule, *"Do unto others as you would have others do unto you,"* all of these problems could be avoided.

Glory was in grave condition on death row when I found her at the shelter. She was deaf, blind, mute, unable to stand, emaciated, missing of teeth, her heart was bad, her thyroid was low, her kidneys were diseased and she was a twelve-year old diabetic. Someone had dumped her because she was in that condition.

On July 10, two months after Cherry passed away, I went back to the pound looking for Ginger's brother who'd been adopted before her, wondering if someone had brought him back to the kennel. Even though Tiger was still in good health, the loss of our other animals left us feeling a little sparse.

After looking through all of the cages, I saw that he wasn't there nor were there any other feline candidates ready for adoption that day. As I was leaving, I got an impulse to take a quick look at the dogs even though I yet wasn't emotionally ready for another canine because I was still mourning Cherry. But as soon as I cracked open the door to the dogs, there she was in the very first cage.

The loud barking of large, agitated dogs echoed through the kennel halls as the attendant went along with his hose to rinse out the cages and wet down the dogs. He arrived at the first cage where I was standing and began to hose down the dog in it. My eyes looked down when I saw that the water pressure from the hose was making the little dog fall and wash around the messy cage. I yelled at him to stop immediately. Fortunately he did.

Then as she shivered and struggled to stand but couldn't lift and steady herself, our eyes met. With a skinny, drawn, extremely sad little face, she looked at me as I read her heart, "Are you going to hurt me too?" My heart broke at the glance and I fell in love with the dog immediately. And I was so surprised to find another beautiful little Pomeranian in such bad shape at the pound.

I inquired about her and they told me she was a female picked up on the street about four days earlier. No one had come to claim her and she had only three more days to stay at the shelter before she would be euthanised. I applied for her rescue but they detailed everything that was wrong with her and said she was really too sick for a safe adoption because she wouldn't live long. But I insisted that I wanted her. However long God intended for her to live I wanted it to be with love, comfort and dignity.

Unfortunately, I couldn't take her that night because the shelter required time to prepare her. I hated walking away and leaving her to spend one more awful night in that hard, soggy cage.

All night long I kept remembering her sad little face and the soulful expression in her eyes. My heart spent that night with her though we were separated physically until the next morning, when I raced over to the shelter to pick her up.

It was a warm, sunny day when I took her home. As soon as I had her in my arms wrapped up in a soft towel, I carried her outside into the sunlight to show her that she had broken free of that prison and that we were going on to a life together. I sat down on the grass hugging her in the sun and cried over her plight for about fifteen minutes. Then I asked God what her name was, when He told me, "Glory." He named her Glory because though life had brought her to undeserved shame, He would bring her to restoration and show His glory in her. Indeed she was my great treasure, a dazzling beauty that I will cherish forever and look eagerly forward to seeing again.

Over that summer she returned to full bloom in such a special way, though we struggled through many storms. When I first brought her home, her heart started racing so fast I thought she was having an attack. I called the vet and he told me to bring her outside and give her a lot of air. I did so while praying fervently. She recovered. I later realized that once she knew she was safely rescued and adopted into a tender loving home that she began to shed her pain and bad memories, which made her heart react.

Glory expressed some of the most endearing gestures I've ever seen in an animal, although each animal is special in his own way. But she was my little miracle dog. Once deaf, now she could hear; once blind, now she could see; and once mute, now she could bark and speak ever so slightly. From being unable to stand, she now danced and skipped all around and we even walked as far as a mile one afternoon together, slowly very slowly. She loved to sit in her fleece basket and watch me cook. Then just as the food was ready, she'd jump up and come over to beg in the cutest way: she'd stand on her hind legs, though they were still weak, and shake her front paws at me while they were crisscrossed. She was very dainty and lady-like yet her enthusiasm overcame her frailty.

When I brought Glory back to show off, the assistants who work at the shelter were amazed at her recovery. They asked me for a picture of her to post up with her dressed in the neon pink leash and harness. She really emerged to be one of the most beautiful dogs I've ever seen. She had extra large eyes full of innocence, wisdom, and watery love; and the most precious nose, like a jewel, and I confess, it was a little oversized for her face, like a juicy peach and chocolate truffle that on the white snout made her look like a fawn.

But she was a very sick little dog who required continual care. Sometimes she'd have to go outside at three in the morning because she wasn't paper trained. So I'd go with her. The simple things were a daily struggle for her, including her bodily functions. Nothing worked quite right; she had a lot of internal damage from her earlier years. And since sometimes she'd stumble into furniture, I never left her alone to be in harm's way; she was with me every wonderful minute. And we had a splendid summer together; I took her all over Long Island, visiting town after town, and shore after shore. Of course, she was a hit wherever she went.

The last weekend in October was warm so we took Glory for a trip to Brooklyn, back to the park where the squirrels lived in the condo. It was a beautiful Sunday and every man and his dog was there walking the mile loop around the grassy field. She had a terrific time and of course so did I; seeing her happy was all the joy I needed.

But Sunday night, she didn't sleep well. She was up pacing around all night and she kept me awake. Early in the morning she kept coming to my bed and nosing my hand. I thought she wanted to go out to relieve herself, but it was something else. I turned to look at her, feeling a bit tired, and said, "What's wrong, Glory? What do you want?" At that moment I looked into her eyes and our souls met in perfect understanding. She was afraid and answered me with unspoken words, "Mommy, I'm afraid, I think I'm going to die today." I kept looking while I answered back, sadly, "Oh, Glory, I'm so sorry. Why do you feel that way?" She walked out of the room.

Glory was chilly that day, and spent most of the day shivering, so I kept her dressed in a fleece coat and hugged her a lot. I made an appointment with the vet for the evening to see if she had a cold and needed some medication or treatment.

That evening the doctor made it clear that her kidneys were failing massively. At this point there really was nothing else I could do to improve her condition. She had extended beyond the reach of prayer as natural causes had staked their claim. Of course, God could have even raised Glory from the dead if He so desired; but in essence, that's what He had already done for us when I first received her. But now her time had come, I knew it and she knew it.

As the vet prepared the injections, one to put her unconscious, then the other to put her to sleep, Glory did the most amazing thing: she began to pray fervently aloud. She was forming words and sentences, not in English, but clearly discernible as prayer in a doggy language. She was lamenting her coming death; she did not want to leave us. She was so happy to have finally found the home she always wanted and now she was going to lose it. If she knew where she was going to, she likely would not have felt so desperately sad. She was also upset about the whole journey that she had to endure, the way other people treated her, the life that she had to live. All of this was pouring forth from her just the way it would flow out of a human being in his last moments of life.

I stayed with her during the procedure to make sure that it was performed in the most gentle of manners. Unfortunately, the vet seemed rushed this time and he wasn't as considerate as he had been in the past. So I had to contend with him over his technique and handling to guarantee that no last minute poke or jab would have its way with her. Strangely, as sick as she was, literally on death's doorstep, she took an unusually long time to die. Glory was full of the Spirit, Who kept her alive in hope through all of her adversity, Who prayed through her in those last moments, and Who filled her with so much love and life, that even death had a fight to claim her.

A year later I prayed asking God to let me see how Glory is now. Then I saw her in the Spirit in a delicate vision, faint but clear, Glory standing in heaven wearing a beautiful, fragrant coat made entirely of little pink flowers woven together. Her expression was sweet and peaceful. I know this is how I will see her again. And every Sunday in Church when we sing, "Glory to God, give Glory to God...," I smile knowing that indeed, I gave Glory to God.

There is a happy ending prepared for all of these animals; it will be a day of reward and restoration provided by God that will wipe away all of the neglect and suffering they had to endure while in our care or lack thereof.

There are many passages in Scripture that speak of animals in heaven. We are told of horses and angelic creatures like, Seraphim and Cherubim, whose faces resemble animals. Jesus is likened to two animals when He is referred to as the "Lamb of God" and the "Lion of Judah." And we are told that in the millennial kingdom, a period of 1,000 years when Christ will rule the Earth from David's throne in Jerusalem, that the lion will lay down with the lamb in perfect harmony and peace. Now there is great symbolic significance in all of this, such as the reconciliation of the two aspects of Christ, and there is also a literal meaning.

But how can we know if these verses refer to newly-created animals or to those who were redeemed from the earth? I believe that it refers to both, because in order for there to be perfect peace, restoration, and everlasting equilibrium, God must balance the books and account for the fate of every life. Even the slightest residual injustice would tip the scales and prevent the establishment of peace. This is one of the reasons why we never arrive at true peace on earth: because our form of justice is always imperfect and the scales are never righted.

The issue of justice connects to the temporal realm where time often serves as a deciding factor. When creating the universe, God rolled time out of the timeless realm like a giant canvas upon which would be painted growth, change, and progress. In the timeless eternal realm, these functions of change cease to occur as we know them. And it is in the pursuit of these creative processes that living beings exercise their free will to choose good or evil.

Right now in the supernatural realm, there are animals that are like angels in that they have spirit bodies and they have never walked in the flesh. There are also redeemed animals who have obeyed the laws that God instilled in them and have thereby been received into heaven after death. Only God can decide which animals are acceptable for His kingdom and which ones must be rejected based upon His decrees and standards.

I cry when people abuse animals and drive them to sin. But I take comfort in the fact that the Scripture affirms, *"God knows every sparrow that"* *"falls from the sky."* I trust and believe that God is watching every misdeed committed against them, and He will weigh it all in the balance when He calls for the ultimate accounting from each living being that passes on. If human beings who've been granted power, sovereignty, and every functional advantage over animals deliberately or irresponsibly cause them to sin because of maltreatment, you can be sure that the animal will receive mercy but that the person would be dealt with severely.

However it's also true that if an animal obeys the voice of Satan, such as: a well-cared for dog that becomes jealous when a baby is brought home, and attacks that human baby to cause him harm, it is required that the animal be put to death, humanely. Its life must be forfeited for its grievous act, then its soul would be routed by God who knows all things and judges if the animal acted out of illness, such as a brain tumor, or out of malice and disobedience.

Truly, if this were not the case, then there would be no peace in heaven. But thank God, divine justice always does prevail. The Scripture pledges, *"Though weeping endures for the night, joy comes in the morning."* And, *"His punishment is for a season, but His mercy endures forever."*

God also warns that there will be harsh punishment brought down upon anyone who causes a helpless or innocent person or creature to suffer needlessly. This is to be taken seriously. It is also extremely important for offenders to be sternly penalized by the law of the land. For if the law of the land fails to provide justice for victims, both animal and human, then the law of God will come forth, and that's when judgments begin to fall. God has entrusted these responsibilities to us, but when we fail to meet them, He moves in on behalf of those who have been wronged by a corrupt system.

The Scripture says that it would be better for a person to do away with himself than to harm one of the Lord's little ones. The term, "little ones," has three meanings: first, it applies to young children; second, it applies to believers who are either young or simple in their faith; third, it applies to anyone or anything that is as helpless as a child, including the animals. Jesus says that such an injurious person who causes harm to His little ones would suffer less punishment at his own hand than at the just hand of God. The Lord will not take lightly the harming of any of His little ones, human or animal.

Last year a reality television show had two horrible episodes that demonstrated this point quite well. On one show a man was goaded to chase after a boar and knife him to death on camera. The action was supposed to illustrate what living in the wild is like and what one would have to do to survive. But the truth is that it was a horrid, sadistic, cruel pagan rite of animal sacrifice offered up for ratings.

I suppose that the producers and the actor assumed that only fans were watching that episode; but too bad for them as God was also watching and He brought justice down quickly. It was either the very next episode or one shortly thereafter that the man who murdered the animal was standing around a burning caldron when he fell into it on camera. Likely for the thrill of the moment and the ratings, no one else helped him with immediacy. The result was that his hand was burned off.

Though I did not watch these programs but read about the incidents and saw the photos in the newspaper, I can assure you that this is only one highly visible example of God intervening to bring justice when human beings have so miserably failed.

In the same way that punishment applies to both man and beast, so does reward. If not, the character of God would be inconsistent, which it is not. There are many occasions when God instructed the Israelites not to do something by warning that if they disobeyed there would be major consequences. When the Ark of the Testimony was transported through the wilderness, God warned both men and animals not to touch it under any circumstances. Now we don't know how God communicated directly with the animals, but we do know that they were under the guidance auspices of the people who were to control them. As it happened if an animal stumbled and leaned against it, the life of the beast was taken, which was the same judgment imposed upon the people who touched it. The same physical action received the same physical punishment.

There is a similar principle operating in the spiritual realm. Now we don't know every word that God has whispered into the ears of animals; but we certainly have many instances recorded, both in the Bible and in news sources, which clearly demonstrate that God has used, and continues to use, His animals as messengers.

We know that Jonah was swallowed up by a whale that was directed by the Lord, and that the rebellious prophet Balaam rode on a donkey that was able to see an angel standing before him, and afterward turned around and spoke to the prophet in his native tongue asking, *"Why are you kicking me?"* This demonstrates the awareness level of the animal as well as his innate ability to recognize and respond to the spiritual realm as God enabled him.

Every day there is a new story to be included among the numerous incidents reported of animals coming to the rescue of people. How would they know to do this if God did not tell them? Because some of these stories are intensely dramatic and far surpass the explanation of instinct alone. And how could they hear God if they did not have a spiritual capacity? The fact is that they could not if they did not.

One such remarkable story happened to an elderly man in Connecticut. A storm was rolling in and the man was tinkering around in his outdoor workshop. Gray, ominous clouds had blown across the sky rapidly, but the rain, thunder, and lightning had not yet begun. John, the older gent, walked over to an old car parked in the lot and sat inside digging around for some tools in the glove box. The car was parked next to a metal fence.

At the same time, his dog was way across a field digging around in the dirt. John kept puttering around until he finally found what he was looking for. Then he attempted to climb out of his car when suddenly, his dog charged across the field into the lot and chomped into John's sleeve and dragged him back into the vehicle. Immediately, a strong bolt of lightening hit the metal fence where John was just about to touch. He would have been instantly electrocuted. The dog knew in advance and saved his owner's life.

There are many such stories of faithful life-saving animals. One of my favorites would be the one when a crippled little boy fell into a river where his parents couldn't save him in time, and a seal appeared from nowhere and lifted the boy onto the shore. Previously, it was recorded that there were no seals known to visit or live anywhere near that river.

Yet we still don't fully recognize what a wonderful partnership we make with our fellow creatures. The Prophet Habakkuk in 2:17 wrote, *"The violence you have done to Lebanon will overwhelm you, and the destruction of animals will terrify you."*

Clearly God is going to judge us for the way we have treated His animals. After all, we may have temporary guardianship over them, but He owns them. They are all His. In fact we are told in Scripture that the animals will praise and honor God for His goodness.

Certainly they cannot do this if they die in this life at the hands of some cruel master without glimpsing their own vindication and justice. They also cannot do this if they subsequently disappear into nothingness when they die. Nothingness does not exist as a post-incarnate state anyway; it is only a theoretical concept with no genuine or verifiable validity. In actuality there is no such thing as nothingness. It is merely a term used to fill a void of understanding, because even a vacuum in space is something – it is a vacuum in space. Therefore if animals have souls, then those souls cannot go into nothingness, they must go somewhere else.

Now it's also argued that animals are simply physical creatures who perish in their entirety when they die and that no part of them remains other than their molecules which are ultimately recycled into the food chain. However, as I stated previously, if this were true, then they couldn't respond to spirits, which they do. Rather they would be devoid of such comprehension and exchange, including the ability to fulfill the Word when they praise God, which is what all creatures were created for.

The animals possess the same breath of life that people do as they are living beings. They have living souls that we commune with non-verbally for the most part. Think of it this way, if you sent out signals into a desolate region of the universe that had no equipment to pick up your communication, or no objects and substance to bounce off of, you would receive no response. Yet profound responses are received when a person sends out a soul-to-soul signal to an animal, which proves he has to have the equipment to receive and transmit – behold, a living soul is resident within that special creature.

I believe that we are deliberately not told of the precise destiny of animals as a means of testing our integrity, while He watches how we treat them. God has deliberately not spelled out the complete details about the afterlife of animals for this reason: if people were certain that other created beings went to heaven, then they might be even more inclined to mistreat or disregard them thinking that it doesn't matter what happens to them on Earth because God will pick up the slack in heaven.

It might also tempt man to try to play God with the eternal destiny of animals and find ways to condemn them eternally. But God, in His infinite wisdom and knowledge of the wicked ways of man, has kept this power and insight from us.

There are other reasons why we are not told directly. It is recorded that Jesus was asked about the future of the Apostle John, to which He replied, *"What's it to you if he remain until I come?"* This means that God has an individual sovereign plan for every person: human, animal, and angelic, and that it is no one else's business what He decrees fair for another one.

A woman asked Jesus if He could position her sons favorably in the afterlife which the Lord promptly explained that these things are appointed by the Father and are not up for grabs or arranged as political favors. The point here is that we will never know exactly how God will judge another, whether he is man or beast. This simply is not our affair.

The good side of this fact is that man cannot manipulate the eternal destiny of animals because he hasn't the knowledge to do so. The bad side is that not knowing the ultimate outcome of our own animals, or those for whom we feel great empathy, leaves us feeling sad over those we've lost and can only hope to see again someday. But let me increase that hope by saying that it's the rare and particularly vicious animal that misses redemption; whereas the vast majority of human beings will miss it, which is so hard to accept, yet a stark and blazing truth, the very one that Christ died so horribly for.

God judges the sins of animals according to the standards He gave to every species relative to the conditions under which each would have to live. The Scripture makes a distinction between "clean" and "unclean" animals. After the flood, this was the premise upon which God determined what was permissible for humans to eat. Though the decisions were made upon certain characteristics, like the shape of the creatures' hooves, unclean animals were basically those who ate unclean things or who participate in violent practices, such as scavenging or carnivorism.

The reason for this relates to the shedding of blood and the fact that these kinds of animals were not suitable for Temple sacrifice. Additionally when an animal is consumed for food, the last moments of its life are taken in along with its meat, which can make the devourer unclean from the consumption of violence, suffering, fear, and decay. This depends on a variety of circumstances. We know that the Prophet Daniel was forbidden to eat any of the King's rich food because it was sacrificed to foreign gods and defiled. For this reason and others, we need to pray over all of our foods before eating them because we don't know under what conditions they were harvested and what they may contain.

In addition to that we must give thanks for all the lives that have been taken so that we can eat and live. When we eat animal foods, do we stop to pray and thank God for His provisions and the great sacrifice of the animals? Do we wonder about the animals, under what circumstances they were forced to surrender their bodies for our bodies? Do we rejoice knowing these creatures have been redeemed and that someday we may thank them face-to-face?

What about the people who hold jobs that require them to kill animals every day? Do we pray that God keep them from sin? Do we beseech God to place mercy in their hearts so that they will treat the animals with dignity and kindness even in these harshest of circumstances? Do we pray for the souls of these people who are daily splattered in blood, that they do not become tainted by bloodlust and find themselves in danger of eternal judgment? If we don't, we should.

And we should also pray for the courageous defenders of animals, that they do not adopt anti-social or destructive measures to win their battles for advocacy and deliverance. These compassionate and brave souls need our prayers daily because they carry the heavy burdens of the animals very close to their hearts, and sometimes these troubles are too heavy to bear. Most of us are insulated from the real heartache of the animals; but the rescuers have to see it on the frontlines then live with the images.

I personally cherish all of these rescuers and believe their causes to be noble and God-directed. I've met people whose entire lives were devoted to rescuing one type of an animal or another, and I've been pleased to assist them on several occasions. One man I know goes into the worst neighborhoods to rescue large, dangerous dogs that have been used for fighting. When I was in college, I worked with an organization that was rescuing whales, seals, and dolphins. And I've assisted with others, which sometimes includes the rescuing of the rescuer.

The Apostle Peter wrote that *"brute beasts"* are *"born for destruction."* Here he makes a dual point: that some animals are made for rough, brute purposes, and he also likens brutal people to these types of beasts. This passage does not refer to all animals, which some people have misinterpreted. Clearly, a baby lamb is not such a brute beast, as all people are not brutal. But in each category there are individual animals who are obedient and responsive versus those who are rebellious and vicious. It is also written that *"some are made for noble purposes while others are made for ignoble purposes."* This is a deep concept and difficult to understand but it is true for both man and beast.

The Prophet Ezekiel writes in 34:15-22 *"I will feed My flock and I will lead them to rest, declares the Lord God; I will seek the lost, bring back the scattered, bind up the broken, and strengthen the sick; but the fat and strong I will destroy. I will feed them with judgment. And as for you, My flock, thus says the Lord God, "Behold, I will judge between one sheep and another; between the rams and the male goats. Is it too slight a thing for you that you should feed in the good pasture, that you must tread down with your feet the rest of your pastures? Or that you should drink of the clear waters, that you must foul the rest with your feet?"*

Continuing, *"And as for My flock, they must eat what you tread down with your feet, and they must drink what you have fouled with your feet!"*

"Therefore, thus says the Lord God to them, Behold I even I will judge between the fat sheep and the lean sheep. Because you push with flank and with shoulder and thrust at all the weak with your horns, until you have scattered them abroad. Therefore I will deliver my flock, and they will no longer be prey; and I will judge between one sheep and another."

What is stated here applies simultaneously to both humans and animals. This is a behavior that God despises and one that He will judge harshly. Whether this is manifest by greedy, self-seeking spiritual leaders, abusive authorities, competitive or domineering individuals or gluttonous animals, God warns that He is aware of these deeds and that He will not let these injustices slip by without imposing appropriate penalties. In this passage, God is setting aside the behavior of some animals as a cautionary example for us to learn from and heed His advice.

Also this passage clearly states that God will bring the animals into account for their actions; and it reveals the mystery regarding His covenant with them. Here we see that they have been instructed in their own languages and by the internal instilling of God's will, not to be selfish, greedy, and destructive toward one another or against God's creation as a whole. We can observe some animals behaving this way, pushing and shoving each other out of reach to get a better chance at survival. God is stating that this is not pleasing in man or in beast, because He is the One Who establishes and sustains all life, and to behave like this is to disobey, doubt, and disrupt His plan and His capacity to provide. Self-reliance leads to self-will which leads to self-centeredness, all of which carry us farther away from God's presence.

One night, I had a childlike dream during which I saw heavenly animals, though I do not know if they were of the angelic variety or of the redeemed collection. As I slept, my room appeared to take on a supernatural quality. Light entered the room first through a small hole in the wall against the floor. It was like a mouse hole. Then four little, white, luminous animals walked in one by one. They were cute and adorable. They didn't look like regular animals, they were spiritual and pure.

The first one to enter was a baby hamster; the second was a duckling; the third was a squirrel, and the fourth was a toddling rabbit. They entered the room walking as though they were marching in a "happy parade." And there was music playing that appropriately kept in step with their entrance and movements.

During the dream I knew that I was seeing a secret about heaven and about the spiritual nature of animals. I could feel their pure and gentle love as they came over and encircled me. Animals are able to speak the language of heaven, which is love, and often it is pure, unbiased, unconditional and faithful. This is the language of the Spirit and the language of God when He speaks to His children.

We are also called to speak this language to one another as well as to the animals. But we have become so preoccupied that we often fail to do so. For this reason our relationships crumble: because we have stopped bathing our actions and expressing our thoughts in love. This is a choice that we are called to make every time we reach out to another soul and each time we part our lips to speak. The Scripture teaches that if we have all things but do not have love, that we really have nothing.

One reason for this is because the only thing we can take with us when we die is love. Everything else will remain behind in the perishing world. The only eternal investment we can make on earth must be made in love. Acts of love done in faith and hope will remain forever, as they are transported like an offering of incense up to God in heaven.

It is written, *"Love never fails."* And I add to that, faith never dies. And what is faith, but a translation of love in a yearning and trusting heart. In Hebrews 11:1-3 we read, *"Now faith is the assurance of things hoped for, the conviction of things not seen. For by it the men of old gained approval. By faith we understand that the worlds were prepared by the Word of God, so that what is seen was not made out of things which are visible."*

Love preceded faith and in the end faith will terminate in perfect fulfilled love. But for now, faith acts as a vehicle that transports us into the presence of God's love, without which, we will not be able to pass beyond the veil of our comprehension to grasp both what is required of us as well as what has been promised to us.

It was by faith and love that St. Francis of Assisi (early 12th Century) preached to the animals. The love he held in his heart for God opened him up to feel such a profound empathy with all creatures that his understanding grew; it deepened to such an extent that he became able to communicate directly with the animals and they would respond.

St. Francis felt he had a mission to instruct the animals to praise their Creator, after all that is what they were brought to life for. In this oneness with nature, Francis in his humble observance was able to discover spiritual truths about creation that were hidden from all of his contemporaries.

We often tend to think of God in exclusively divine or supernatural terms and forget how natural He is, having created all that is in nature. In fact every structure, force, element, or creature we find in nature in some way reflects a special attribute of its Designer, the master Architect of the universe.

Francis of Assisi apprehended this oneness, the unity of the Creator's original intention for His complete family. However this is a condition that will not be known again in full until all who are destined for heaven join Him there. Another promise is that a new earth will be created after the old one has been destroyed. And it is in this new earth that the original order will be restored as the devil will have been done away with permanently. How sweet and wonderful will be that day!

"For I consider that the sufferings of this present time are not worthy to be compared with"

"the glory that is to be revealed in us. For the anxious longing of the creation waits eagerly for the revealing of the sons of God. For the creation was subjected to futility, not of its own will, but because of Him who subjected it, in hope that the creation itself also will be set free from its slavery to corruption into the freedom of the glory of the children of God. For we know that the whole creation groans and suffers the pains of childbirth together until now. And not only this, but also we ourselves, having the first fruits of the Spirit, even we ourselves groan within ourselves, waiting eagerly for our adoption as sons, the redemption of our body." Romans 8:18-23

We know that a dreadful day is coming when the world will become very dark and that the light of God will be squeezed out by the last works of the devil. As this terrible time approaches, worse than any other in history, the groaning of creation will increase, for it suffers greatly under the yoke of evil.

But we also know that all of creation will praise and bless the Lord: *"Praise the Lord from the earth, sea monsters and all deeps; fire and hail, snow and clouds; stormy wind, fulfilling His Word; mountains and all hills; fruit trees and all cedars; beasts and all cattle; creeping things and winged fowl; kings of the earth and all peoples; princes and all judges of the earth; both young men and virgins; old men and children. Let them praise the name of the Lord, for His name alone is exalted; His glory is above earth and heaven."* Psalm 148:7-13

78

We are even told that *"the trees of the fields will clap their hands"* in praise of God. This may be difficult for us to imagine, but they will do it in their own way as God has enabled them.

Last year I first became acquainted with the sensitive awareness of trees, that if I didn't see it myself, I would have found it difficult to believe. I have always loved and been fascinated by trees, they are like wise sentinels, historians who observe and record, but only interfere on rare occasion. I have felt their presence in an organic way, but never realized that perhaps they also felt mine.

Unfortunately, in my neighborhood the new people moving in do not like anything that grows except grass. So they cut everything down, and if they replant anything, it's always a pigmy version. When I first moved here four years ago, there were lush greens and tall trees all around. Since that time many have been removed, at least a third of what was around, though I still have and love my twenty-two trees, and apart from any impending tropical storm, intend to keep them as long as they remain healthy.

But last year when my neighbor went after his oak tree, I saw an amazing thing happen. The oak was in the center of his lawn, and he claimed, it was blocking the sun, though the family is never home during the day to enjoy it. Right before the choppers arrived I walked over and sat outside with another neighbor to enjoy the spring breeze; then an army of trucks came and a platoon of saws piled out.

Now this was a good-looking, healthy oak that always produced a robust flourish in season; but it also yielded a hearty leaf fall at harvest, which opposes the comfort zone of suburban paunch. So for this and other offenses, it was about to be cut down. But here's when an amazing thing happened and I saw it.

While sitting with my neighbor, I turned to see what all the noise was about when I saw another tree move by itself. It was a maple planted at the far north corner of their property about twelve feet from the doomed tree. When the red oak was half destroyed, the maple tipped over in what I can only describe as a gesture of great, personal sorrow. At that moment I saw something in the Spirit: that trees have some kind of awareness and feelings, that they care for one another, and that they have some kind of tree soul which is capable of mourning, and as the Scripture says, praising God.

We have all seen pictures of animals, such as elephants, standing over their dead loved ones and mourning with strong emotions. But trees? Yes, trees, the elephants of the green world. Standing alone and unloved, the maple began to die; and a few months later, my neighbor cut down his last tree. I wasn't home at the time, but saw the stump when I returned.

Of course, my computer is seated on a wood desk which once was a tree, a maple, in fact. And the paper I print out my manuscripts on also came from my friends, the trees. But my hope is that the life that I lead and the purposes of my usage will be noble enough to honor the sacrifice they all had to make in order for me to reach humanity for God. In this way, the little poem may be fulfilled: "Upon the pressed fibers of a tree, I etched my story passionately; for once it stood with immobile girth, but now will travel across the earth."

God is the ultimate conservationist and He will let nothing go to waste that can be redeemed; so even the trees have a provision in His eternal plan. And they are also spoken of in Scripture as having special significance, like the two great prophets of the last days who are called, "two olive trees," and when *"Jesus saw Nathanael coming to Him, and said of him, "Behold, an Israelite indeed, in whom is no guile! Nathanael said to Him, "How do You know me?" Jesus answered and said to him, "Before Philip called you, when you were under the fig tree, I saw you.""* John 1:47-48

Most of the references of fig trees in the Bible are used as analogs for Israel and the Jewish people. Trees are supposed to give off their fruit and Israel was supposed to be a family tree that bore the fruit of the Spirit reliably to every successive generation. But as we discussed earlier, the canopy of the tree also symbolized the presence of God.

Jesus also likened Himself to a plant saying, *"I am the vine, and My Father is the vinedresser. Every branch in Me that does not bear fruit, he takes away; and every branch that bears fruit, He prunes it, that it may bear more fruit."*

The passage continues, *"You are already clean because of the word which I have spoken to you. Abide in me, and I in you. As the branch cannot bear fruit of itself, unless it abides in the vine, so neither can you, unless you abide in Me. I am the vine, you are the branches; he who abides in Me, and I in him, he bears much fruit; for apart from Me you can do nothing. If anyone does not abide in Me, he is thrown away as a branch, and dries up; and they gather them, and cast them into the fire, and they are burned."* John 15:1-6

And when one does not abide in Him, we are told in another passage, *"It has made My vine a waste, and My fig tree splinters. It has stripped them bare and cast them away; their branches have become white.*

"Wait like a virgin girded with sackcloth for the bridegroom of her youth. The grain offering and the libation are cut off from the house of the Lord. The priests mourn the ministers of the Lord the field is ruined the land mourns for the grain is ruined the new wine dries up. Fresh oil fails. Be ashamed, O farmers, Wail O vinedressers, for the wheat and the barley; because the harvest of the field is destroyed.

"The vine dries up, and the fig tree fails; the pomegranate, the palm also, and the apple tree, all the trees of the field dry up. Indeed rejoicing dries up from the sons of men." Joel 1:7-12

A few years back while walking Cherry, I came upon a vine that had grown along a sycamore. The vine grew all around the trunk and up into one of the tree's largest branches. Over the summer the vine choked off the natural leaves of that branch and replaced them with itself. This was a perfect illustration of how the Lord wants to be in our lives; He is the vine that needs to wrap around us, fill us, and replace our old egos, self-will, and carnal drives with His divine purpose and loving guidance.

Each and every day, the divine Word of God is actively working all around us and it forms the basis for all natural law. Every scientific principle has a correlation in Scripture and every observable phenomenon can be understood in Biblical terms. In the years to come, I hope and believe that many of these mysteries will be revealed because the generation of our modern world needs to hear them. But for now we can rejoice knowing that God is not only seated upon His throne in supernatural heaven, but He's also in the hearts of His redeemed children and in addition, can be found in the essence of His creative attributes present everywhere abounding in His natural world.

Jesus presented His divine wisdom in stories, parables, and teachings by including various aspects of nature. He'd always draw a link between heaven and earth because He, Himself, was that link, as all things came from Him and connect back to Him. And when He says that He cares for and guides all things, even the little birds, His Word is reliable.

Every year on the first day of spring, I watch the Lord's Word proven true yet again. Perhaps if I have forgotten to look at my calendar, I might not remember what day it is at first, but before the morning clears into noon, Angelo is quick to remind me with loud chirping from atop my mailbox.

A family of Cardinals took a liking to my house; perhaps it was the sunflower seeds, bread, or wild bird food that attracted them. Or maybe it was set in just the right spot amidst my humble forest to make them feel at home. But whatever it is, every thaw, they arrive with a gregarious announcement.

I love little, red Angelo. He has shown such intelligence and understanding in the four years that I've known him. Whatever room in the house I may be in at the moment, if he wants my attention he comes right to that window and chirps by the sill, sometimes even pecking on the glass. I still can't figure out how he can sense where I am when I'm out of sight. But his favorite spot is the picnic table in front of my house where I regularly feed him.

Last year a crow came against his nest when either an egg was hatching or a chick was weaning. I heard the battle raging out my window about six o'clock in the morning. The crow was squawking loudly which woke me up, and then I heard Angelo chirping back frantically. I knew my boy's voice and jumped out of bed only to see the crow facing off against Angelo by the nest.

The only thing I could groggily think of was to yell, but it didn't work. I reached out and banged on the roof near the tree, but that didn't stop the fight. So I grabbed for a rubber band and snapped it passed the crow, which scared him off. But he came back again and battled for about forty-five minutes until I finally chased him for good. I threw some food out for him, and perhaps after he repaired his self-image, he ate what was available.

About two months later, Angelo came to the picnic table and presented his young one to me. He jumped up with more than his usual enthusiasm and chirped by the front window. This was the cutest thing ever: there he stood proudly with his plumes slightly puffed out presenting his son to me, the one that I had rescued. As they stood side-by-side, I knew that they thanked me, so they ate extra well that morning. And though I have kept the sparrows afloat all winter, I once again eagerly await the return of Angelo and his extended family.

I've had so many precious, tender moments of communion with the animals. We just have to know how to read them. But if we love and respect them, our hearts will open up to all that they have to share with and teach us. And if all that we are able to learn from them is how to be sensitive to the needs and individuality of others, then that understanding alone is a worthy message and one that we all need to hear.

Apples increased my understanding in this regard, and I hope to see her again though she left one night without a trace. For a few weeks my cats Ginger and Sparrow did not come to bed; they were staying up all night and pouncing at the tall, back window that looks into the yard. At first, I thought they were playing with each other. Then I looked out and saw the opossum. She had come to eat the food left over from the other animals.

At first she only sniffed it, shy and timid about even approaching it, then she put her head down with a sad facial expression and walked away thinking: "That couldn't possibly be for me. I'm a possum; nobody loves me. They think I'm ugly and are afraid of me. I better leave it alone." I watched her expressions out the window. Then I said under my breath, "You're not ugly, you're adorable! And I love you. Now come and eat, that potato bread is for you. Go take it and come back for more."

Just then the possum returned, looked around and took the slice then waddled away with it. But the sweetest part was the smile on her face and the twinkle I saw in her eye. Now I know she didn't hear me, but I believe that the Holy Spirit carried my message to her providing a much needed touch from God.

The animals can feel forsaken too, and they pray asking God for provision, direction, and mercy. How wonderful it is when we can be a part of that relationship and strengthen their faith and hope, and increase their joy. Apples remained with me for six months, heartily eating in the back yard, as my cats eagerly looked for her nocturnal appearing. But one night before the winter set in, she finished her piece of apple and approached the window looking in at me. She put her head down as if to bow, the look in her eyes was a bit nervous and retiring, and I sensed in that moment that she was saying, "I'll be leaving you now. Thank you for all you gave me." I felt sad because at that moment she looked so vulnerable out there and I knew there was nothing I could do for her. That was her habitat; she was not meant to be inside safe and warm, but out there among all the rest who are entrusted to God.

As it turned out that was the last night that I ever saw Apples. Sparrow and Ginger miss her and still run to the window every night hoping to catch her foraging about. I've called the wildlife center to try to find out what happened to her, but there are several possibilities when it comes to opossum. She could have moved onto another feeding ground, as they are nomadic by nature. Or she could have been pregnant and left to wean her young, since they are marsupials. Or she could have passed away because they only live a few years; their natural life spans, even in captivity, are very short. But whatever the case, I love my pet possum and know that someday I will see her again.

But the stories of animal awareness, feeling, and sensitivity are endless. One hot Sabbath day while walking to my friend's Sephardic synagogue in Brooklyn, I came upon a worm stuck on a dry, parched pavement. I tend not to feel so comfortable around squiggly things like worms, but this one needed my help. If it would have stayed there, it would have dried up and burned on the concrete, with an army of ants hungrily waiting. I found a twig and inched the worm onto it. When I put the worm down on the dewy shaded grass, it rejoiced and with visible renewal danced away to safety. I thought to myself, my God, even a lowly worm can rejoice and have feelings.

Over the years whatever animal came my way, I cared for it accordingly. If it was domestic, I would adopt it; if it was wild, I would make sure it went into the best possible environment in the best of health. These have included mice, birds, cats, dogs, squirrels, deer, seals, raccoons, butterflies and caterpillars, chipmunks, turtles, tortoises, otters, and several others including certain insects. Each one of these cases has a touching story associated with it and a passing relationship that ran deep between us.

The last one that I will share with you is that of Lisa. In the fall of 1984, I moved into a cabin in Connecticut. I wanted some artistic isolation, a private place of contemplation where inspiration could visit me. At this time, I didn't believe in God but I was searching for truth higher than myself.

Around mid-December I began to undergo a succession of hardships. My car broke down and I couldn't get to work, so I lost my job. And the first troubling symptoms of Diabetes took hold, though I didn't know what caused the health problems. Then a week before Christmas, I was cleaning around the closet when a small Cabbage White butterfly gently fluttered out into the room and perched itself on the wall where I was standing.

I looked her over at first thinking that it was a moth; but upon careful examination I saw that she was a little, white butterfly who was hiding from the winter's chill. So now I had a roommate. We had a lot of fun together but also shared moments of peril. It seemed like everywhere I went in the cabin, Lisa was in some kind of immediate danger that I needed to save her from.

One time she landed in the open bowl which I almost flushed with her in it. Another time during a shower she landed on the edge where the water droplets were hitting all around her. Still on another occasion, I turned on the bathroom vent and she almost got sucked into it. For some reason she liked the bathroom and would stay in there most of the time. So that is where I'd feed her and spend a little time together.

The sweetest moment was one time when I was washing my face she was perched on the edge of the sink watching me. As I dried my face with the towel, I looked over at her and saw that she was using her front legs to wash her face just as I was doing. We had gotten this close.

Lisa lasted until Christmas, but the day after she began to die. Her energy was quickly running down and she couldn't move from her spot on the sink anymore. I called a local vet but she said it was probably the end of the butterfly's tiny life span. So all I could do now was just to speak to Lisa and tell her how much I loved her and thanked her for being my Christmas butterfly, a messenger of God's love, sweetness, and beauty, a message that touched and opened my unbelieving heart.

Years before, while driving on a long stretch of California freeway, I came upon a stretch that cut through two fields: the section on the west side of the road was filled with wildflowers, and in the east section, acres of butterflies, mostly Cabbage Whites, were fluttering about. But as the butterflies tried to cross the busy roadway to get to their food supply, the wildflowers, they were being blown about by the wind of passing cars and trucks and knocked to the ground. Most were being hit by the vehicles, and only a rare attempt was resulting in a successful migration. All of the others, many thousands, lay dying on the blacktop.

Seeing this, I pulled my car over and went into the middle of the road. Honestly, I don't know how I got away with this, but for two hours I stayed there picking up the little Whites and gently carrying those that were alive over to the flowers. I don't know how many I had rescued before circumstances drove me on, but it was a large number.

Admittedly, this was the most dangerous and eccentric thing that I have ever done on behalf of animal life; but the situation touched my heart in an instant, and I acted on it. Though for the sake of your safety, I don't recommend this to you.

Nevertheless, when Lisa, the same type of butterfly, came to me years later, I took it as a sign of appreciation for having esteemed the helpless and small at the risk of my own life. It was in essence, as if one of the Cabbage Whites from that California group came back to say thanks with a kiss of love.

Also in some ways, I suppose it was the symbolism of the butterfly that grabbed me on the highway that day. Butterflies metamorphose. They change into glorious, delicate, little flying animals with beautiful coloration, from fuzzy caterpillars that struggle along on the earth against many odds and adversaries in valiant efforts to crawl up the nearest tree and enter their cocoons.

We are like the caterpillar in this life as we strive to survive and climb the tree of success and happiness. And when we place our lives in Christ, it is like entering the cocoon where He will transform us from simple travelers on difficult paths into magnificent treasures that exude God's beauty with loft and grace. And in its final stage as the butterfly, this little animal represents how we will be renewed in our new lives in heaven: exquisite and sweet, free and easy forevermore.

Inside every caterpillar is a butterfly waiting to emerge. But only with God's love and nurturing will these come forth. This is also true for every relationship that we have for the Lord's miraculous transforming power knows no limits. We set these boundaries in our unbelief; but with faith, they can be overcome. For it's only by the exponential power of love that the invisible becomes visible to provide a depth of visual field that is otherwise unattainable; and it enables us to gain wisdom that is exclusively granted to those who move within this supernatural substance. Without love and faith the door to higher truth will remain forever closed.

91

Yesterday while in the midst of another love fest of delights, this hidden door opened to me yet again. It was while I was meticulously grooming Jesse Merciful. His shimmering, curly, long white fur needed a spring trim. So for over two hours, he rolled about on the toweled sofa as I ever so gently barbered him, not missing any unruly hair nor pulling one accidentally in my enthusiasm to make him even more beautiful than he already was and is.

During our session, I became peacefully lost in his luminous, fluffy white cotton fields, the reams of creamy oyster yarn spun about his hot, pink little body. In my gaze he appeared just like a baby lamb being sheared; and at that moment, as he reclined to present his treasured belly, I was blessed to see Jesus in Jesse.

I also saw that it is so easy for us to love Jesus as a lion, as a conquering king who rules with power and might; but it is so difficult for us to love Him as the Lamb. In part this is because we so often may feel helpless and in need of His divine strength and protection in order to make us feel secure. The last thing many folks would ever want is a God that they would have to protect and tend to the needs of.

For this reason, it's so much easier to "love" a lion; yet when we do so, it is with awe, reverence, and a varying portion of fear, as it is natural to fear that which has deadly potential and overwhelming power. But the irony is that love is more pure when fear is absent, it is more genuine, more intimate, and more fluid flowing with ease and exchanged without obstruction. *"Perfect love casts out all fear."*

This is how Jesus wants us to love Him and that is one of the primary reasons why He revealed Himself like a lamb. In this He put Himself on such a humble and tender footing that when we come to Him as such, it is on the most pure, tender, and heart-to-heart basis without any impeding status, any elite demeanor, any repelling trepidation, or any thing that would separate Him from those He loves. The Lord wants us to love His sweetness, purity, delicateness, fineness, softness, lovingkindness, and sentimentality just as much as His valor, nobility, courage, fortitude, majesty, righteousness, power, mastery, and His other victorious attributes.

Many of us are afraid of the vulnerability this brings; but know this, no matter how strong you may feel, or how imposing you think you need to be, the only real might you'll ever have, which can never be taken away or destroyed, is the power of the Lord and the strength of His might. And when we hold onto Him in love and faith, no matter what happens around us or to the outward part of us, it means little or nothing because the inner and eternal part cannot be destroyed when it clings to the Lord in love.

It is this same indestructible love that carried Jesus through His awful ordeal all the pain-filled way to victory, the same victory He has planned for all who follow goodness in the light of His way, for He is "the truth, the life, and the way." And yes, he also loves His animals more than we can imagine.

After about a seasonal year embraced in our loving care, Jesse Merciful began to show signs of loneliness for one of his own. He'd get very excited and whimper, bark, bleat, oink, and snort every time we'd pass another little dog he wanted to play with.

No matter how hard you try, there's really no adequate replacement for the companionship of one on the same "nose level" as oneself. It is true that some animals prefer to be an only pet, but most, like Jesse, are social, and they long for a likeminded friend to share life, love, adventure, and food with.

In my search to find Jesse Merciful a female, a little sister of like breed, age, personality, and size, I located several kind rescue groups with adoptable dogs wearing sad little faces, bearing tearful stories.

Thankfully, though it took several difficult months before I was able to secure one, I found the little girl who seemed to need our love the most. It was destiny, and often, you have to wait for that.

Christie had been rescued from a puppy mill in Missouri where she'd spent her entire life of eight years in a small wire cage. She was forced to have about thirty litters and was very neglected. She had never been held, cuddled, taken for a walk, fed tasty food, or given the chance to play and just be a dog.

A wonderful woman, Arlene Rielle, runs a rescue mission and a foster home with a team of people in various states who go to the mills to redeem the old dogs after they've been used and abused and are in danger of being destroyed. God bless these marvelous people who do this selfless, costly work

94

without pay, who are often in delicate health and circumstances themselves. Arlene, this year, while battling persistent cancer, hired a truck from northern New York to Missouri to rescue fifty-seven dogs, bringing them all back home to prepare for adoption. These rescuers are truly some of the most tender-hearted and genuine people on earth, how they need our prayers, support, and help to care for the money machine's ravaged discards.

This journey alone is also very difficult for the animals and not all of them make it. But this is how I located my Christie Lovejoy, through a series of referrals from one foster rescuer to another.

I had to drive over six hundred miles to pick her up near Syracuse, upstate New York. She was being fostered by Arlene, who takes in and adopts hundreds of rescued dogs each year.

The more I got to know this rescuer, the more I came to love her. While caring tirelessly for the dogs, she is also struggling with a severe illness that keeps threatening to claim her life, yet she presses on and the disease keeps going into remission. God is with His mercy-givers, as Scripture says, *"Blessed are the merciful for they shall obtain mercy."*

Through this adventuresome experience, I came to learn more about the arduous plight of the people who have given their lives to save and care for the animals. The rescuers themselves are often in great peril. Many are ill, live in harsh conditions, struggle financially, are in danger of eviction, are threatened by opponents, and endure broken hearts.

But love knows no bounds, and these people, God bless them, are ruled by love which plays in concert with hope and faith, with love being the highest directive of any motivating force. It is the eternal offering which shall never pass away.

Not knowing which road life will take me on from here, I'm grateful to have been able to adopt at least one more, and to have had perhaps the final story, be one so rich in substance and Spirit. Lord knows, if I could redeem them all, I surely would, but thank God, He has called out and raised up an active network of modern day St. Francis's humble caretakers and servants who have devoted their days to loving and honoring God's creatures both great and small. Let those of us who love animals, join with them in word and deed.

For those who may still doubt that there are animals in heaven, let me assure you that there most certainly are. In some of my other books I recount my unusual spiritual gift in greater detail. Realizing that this gift, being rare and out of the ordinary, is difficult for some to believe, I have left the best for last. With the trust that by the time you have arrived at a deeper level of insight with a sturdy foundation laid, let us take the next step onto a higher plane and into a closer communion with the Lord.

On ten separate occasions, in both dreams and visions, during a seven-year period from 1990 to 1996, I have seen Jesus Christ face-to-face. This is not through any power of my own, but only by God's divine decree for reasons only He knows.

And though I will not describe Jesus here, this is provided in my other book, I will say only that He did not resemble the typical portraits of Him. I did not see Him as He looked on earth, but as He looks now in His glorified presence. And when you see Him, you know that you're not seeing someone who is merely human in the mortal sense, but rather One who is decidedly divine. There is no mistaking His exalted deity, He is the God-man.

On two of the occasions that He appeared to me, there was an animal present. I twice saw the Lord's majestic white warrior horse. The first time was in a dream, when I saw Jesus walk across a lush green meadow to a lone wooden stable where His exquisite-beyond-words, pure, brilliantly-luminous white horse with opalescent eyes, was waiting for Him in perfect peace.

The Lord opened the top portion of the split barn door and the horse came forward and stuck his head out. Jesus stroked him with great love and respect, and then told him something which I was able to hear. Christ said: "We will be going soon." With that, the horse of horses breathed with reverent fury in full and enthusiastic agreement regarding this promised ride. After that, the dream faded.

Then on one other blessed occasion, while preparing a mailing for a charitable project I'd undertaken, I found myself distracted by the beauty of the sky, a vibrant blue gracing the gray cements of the City on a cold winter's day. But with barely a cloud to shroud my entry, I could not resist its charms, and began to daydream. When I was fully captivated, the Lord took me up into the Spirit.

The instrumental music I'd been listening to carried me up to the highest heaven where the veil of eternity opened up and I saw the Lord riding His horse in the highest pasture where no man, not even an angel, could enter into. Instead all who watched Him had to sing upward into that heaven from below where I was positioned in the vision.

In Father's view, this is where Jesus and His horse practice for the day of the great ride, this is where they worship in unison together, where they become one in purpose, and where the victory is expressed in totality before it is brought to earth in finality. And I was watching this in complete awe.

At one point the hidden divide between heaven and earth was removed and I was carried back down to look at the earth, what it will look like when God removes all of the evil from the lower heavens and from the world. I saw a magnificent meadow with a quaint, red farmhouse both radiant with sunlight and resonant with peace and gentility; as timelessly, a sweet calm filled the air like music.

I also saw that when this takes place, there will be no more separation between heaven and earth and we will be able to freely travel from one to the other. This will take place after the devil and his legions of demons and armies of followers are utterly and absolutely destroyed for all eternity. It is the inheritance promised us and God will fulfill it.

The Lord rides His great, noble stallion in valiance and triumph as an exercise for the coming day, that which is soon, my brothers and sisters. Do not find yourselves being robbed of your faith, for *"Satan comes to rob, steal, and destroy"* and *"Marvel not that Satan should come to you as an angel of light."* Don't be deceived in these strange and troublesome days. Know who the true Shepherd is and follow Him only.

Then in the vision, I was carried back up to sing again, upward into the highest pasture and watch the conclusion of the Lord's equestrian event.

When Jesus turned to ride back to the side I was positioned on, He slowed down and the horse began to prance toward me in a kingly exhibition. Though I am a writer, I'm amazed at how difficult it is to find the right words to explain these kinds of spiritual experiences, especially, this one.

But to try, I can only say that at that moment the Lord gave me a look which would be my undoing from that moment on until I join Him in glory. He looked right into me and told me that He loved me and that He knew me completely. He had a look on His face that ruined me forever, in a good way, of course. If I wasn't completely and "madly" in love with Him before that, I surely was by then. And the horse, I want one just like him. He was magnificent.

Then after "that look," Jesus turned on His stallion and rode off with gusto through a series of dewy geysers and an arched rainbow, as the vision became misty and faded.

God is so full of surprises, it's impossible to know all that He has in store. And sometimes when we think the last word has been spoken on an issue, it comes to life again with new poetry and song.

Such is the case of Jeweliette and Jennifurry, our new, petite sister stray cats who'd come to eat and snuggle up next to our house daily until we took them in and made them a cozy place in our family.

In closing, I hope you've come to possess a more complete understanding of God's eternal plan for His animals, and that you've deepened in your personal appreciation for their special attributes. And for those of you who mourn over losing an animal friend, I hope and pray you are comforted by these words and are able to proceed confidently knowing you will see your furry friends in heaven as the teaching of this Book explains.

The Lord has faithfully promised that He will remember forever those among us who are found innocent, faithful, and righteous; and He will not forget their good deeds and tender souls. And if we in our selfish hearts, could find a wellspring of love for the animals; how much more does the Creator, Who is the very personification of love, how much more does He love and care for them.

Therefore, be at peace and put your trust in God; because though some of our beloved pets may have gone they have not been forsaken; and we who walk in faith and love, will surely meet them again. *"Blessed be all who wait for and hope in the Lord for His mercy and love endure forever."*

Visions Of Heaven
A Personal Journey

On ten separate occasions, I've been blessed with supernatural dreams and visions of heaven. The four accounts mentioned earlier in this Book are those that featured animals in them. The other heavenly visions did not, but I'd like to share three more of them with you so that you will know what manner of paradise we will someday enter into.

The first time I had such an experience was in 1984, during a period of staunch agnosticism. On Saturday afternoon, while reclining and listening to some beautiful instrumental music, a glowing cloud misted through my ceiling as I looked up in thought.

The day before this happened, I had visited my mother's cat who was dying from age-related ills. All day and night I lied on my mom's bathroom tile floor beside Keva, who I'd brought home when I was thirteen. Now at twenty-eight and Kevie at sixteen, we had sojourned many years together.

But that afternoon, I was forced to concede that there was nothing more I could do to help her. At this time I didn't know how to pray and didn't believe in God. So all I could do was to give her my love; she showed me how much she had appreciated it by lifting her head and extending her paw onto my hand, while blinking her amber eyes. Moments later, my sweet, orange-striped girl died in my arms.

I was tremendously impacted by this cat's death because of the helplessness we shared in those

101

final hours and the memories we laid to rest forever. Time is so fleeting and it only goes in one direction, forward... but where does it finally come to rest? I wondered. And it goes so quickly, which is why I'm so grateful to God for my precious animal babies as they've provided that "momentary paws" from it all.

On the way home I sat in the passenger seat of our car as James drove from Queens to Brooklyn. Looking at the gray, cold, blustery winter sky I said my first prayer, though at the time, I didn't know it was a prayer, and I had no one particular in mind to whom I was directing it. Nor did I really expect an answer. But when the soul yearns and travails, it will pray within us even when we don't intend to.

Looking up through a break in the clouds where a bright spot in the gloom appeared. Into that dense light patch, I sent up this inquiry: "Is this the total end? Is there anyone out there? Anyone at all? What happens after you die? Do the lights just get shut off and everything turns black? What about life after death? Is this all there is? Can anyone or any thing hear me?"

Only twenty-four hours later, that prayer was answered. While looking up at my living room ceiling in meditation on the music, the cloud of light came in. And from it, I heard one speak in a gentle voice, saying:

"Everything you've ever heard is true. God is true, God is real. There is life after death. Heaven is real; and this is what heaven is like."

Then the cloud began to swirl and pour upon me a misty light, peace, love, exhilaration and joy – a combination of attributes not previously observed together. Looking at it, I said: "WOW!" three times, and on the third time, it faded away.

Instantly I believed! Yet only minutes before I would have considered anyone who had faith to be "a delusional simpleton, an intellectual cripple who needed the crutch of religion to hobble him through the day."

For some reason I jumped up and went over to look in the mirror where I saw light pouring out of my eyes as if they were flashlights in a coal mine.

Amazed by this, but also realizing that I was late to an appointment, I put on my jacket and ran the six blocks to my meeting.

When I arrived four people came over to me inquiring why I was late. In mid-sentence, one man gasped and said, "What happened to you?" Another man said, "Look at her eyes, they look really weird don't they?" Then my brother, James, looked closer and said, "He's right. Go look in the mirror. There's light coming out of your eyes. That's strange. How did that happen?"

When I looked I saw that the light I had first seen in my house mirror had dimmed but that it was still visible and completely unnatural. I was amazed again, and even more amazing, they all saw it too.

My journey from this point became another story altogether with its details contained throughout my ten-volume book series. But along that journey, there were some more heavenly encounters...

One dusk when I was gazing at the sky early in my faith years, I was drawn into the Spirit and I had my first clear vision of heaven.

I saw James sitting in a small wooden boat with me and we were sailing along a beautiful serene river. As the vision progressed, it became more and more extraordinary, supernatural.

There were "happy" trees lining the banks, delicately spaced, and glowing with a radiant light from the inside as though they were lanterns. Each was perfect and symmetrical, waving softly as we passed by. The colors were magnificent, vibrant hues and vivid, shimmering tones hard to describe.

I get "goose bumps" when I recall this part. As we approached a mountain that for a while sat majestically in the distance, our boat followed a curve to the left around the mountain. Just at that moment we entered into an effervescent reservoir where the sun gleamed brilliantly on the water that was bubbling up like champagne. The Spirit within me shot up to meet it like a celebratory firework in an explosion of life that cannot be compared to anything on earth or to anything I've ever seen, heard or imagined.

So much knowledge about heaven and earth rushed into my understanding from this one vision, and specifically, that all of the beautiful things we find here will also be there but in their perfected and "crystallized" state no longer to decay or die.

The last such experience I will recount in this Book came to me in a dream one night.

I saw myself in an emerald-colored meadow standing beside a post-and-beam "horse fence." So I walked along the fence for a while which separated two sections of the rolling green. After a while I came upon a solitary white rose growing near a post which it leaned against. Its fragrance had caught my attention.

When I bent down to sniff its captivating perfume, a man quietly appeared on the other side of the fence and stood beside me. His purple garment appeared in my right peripheral view as my eyes traveled upward to find a "wise man" adorned in a royal robe with a white beard and cottony hair. He began to explain things about life and about God to me in English, which I understood but could not put into words when I awoke, even though I am a writer and words are my life's work.

Somehow the spiritual content of his poetic discourse was not translatable into mortal discussion even though the language uttered was familiar. At this moment I realized that all God has shown us is like 'baby talk' because it is so small compared to all that there is to learn and to know.

As he spoke I noticed something else that was amazing – the words coming out of his mouth looked like spiraling ribbons entirely in poetic verse which is the language of heaven – poetry! This is evidenced in the Bible which is why it is difficult for some people to understand in terms of what is meant to be taken literally or metaphorically and so on. But know this, when God intends for us to take something He spoke metaphorically or symbolically in the abstract, using His poetic license, He provides the interpretation of it directly afterwards so that we won't error in our understanding. Thus, if there is no subsequent interpretation, then the information is meant to be taken literally, as a general rule.

This dream went on for what seemed like hours and had many different scenes. The next one was when he told me to look inside the flower and I did. It drew me in like another dimension full of mysteries and secrets about God and His creation. I was shown that the rose, as well as, everything that God made contains infinite information about itself, about every other thing, and about God. And that all of that information forms a huge, unending lattice of truth composed of love. Even the air particles were made of love, which is not only a feeling, but also a fire, and a divine substance, the glue that holds life together. As Scripture teaches, *"God is love."* (1John)

Later in the dream, James and I were riding on a trolley that wound through mountain towns and villages. Though it had a European look, it was so much more exquisite than anything in existence on Earth, so I knew we were still journeying through some region of heaven.

I was amazed that there will be towns and these kinds of things up there as they are down here, since the idea to create these things in the world have actually come from the eternal realm spiritually pre-existing the building of them into the physical.

I also saw that there are ethereal portals in heaven leading from one realm to the other without a noticeable separation. And these domains seemed endless. But there was a distinction between them, though the mystery of that was not fully revealed to me, just that it has to do with each person's eternal positioning in Christ and his heavenly rewards as in accordance with the Scripture where Jesus says, "In my Father's house there are many mansions."

As we rode along I was shown buildings and even an image of myself, how I will look in heaven.

Little spouts, geysers of mist, were rising up periodically from one realm to another as we passed along certain areas, and I realized that these were the prayers of the believers coming up like incense into the kingdom of glory.

Shortly after this the dream faded to a close, but I will never forget the wonderful journey I went on in the quietude of the deep hours.

Thus, because I was shown how powerful the prayers we send up are and how they become a part of the fabric of heaven, I have concluded this Book with a section of special prayers which I hope and pray that you will read and recite aloud from your heart that we may join together in this holy and sacred mystery for all the good we can do for those we love and those who desperately need our love.

Peace, love, joy, and blessings be forever with you in this life and in the everlasting. Amen.

"The sacrifice of the wicked
Is an abomination to the Lord
But the prayer of the upright
Is His delight."

(Proverbs 15:8)

and

"The Lord has heard my
supplication;
The Lord will receive
My prayer."

(Psalm 6:9)

Prayer For The Animals
And
For People Who Love Them

Almighty God, Giver of life
Father of all creation Have mercy upon me.
Reach down your compassionate and loving hand and
Bless me with healing peace and redemption.
Protect me from harm and guide me
In the light of Your ways and truth.
Blessed Art Thou oh Lord our God,
Creative King of the Universe,
Who reaches out and helps the needy
In his time of sorrow and suffering;
Who comforts those forsaken by this world.
For Lord, my God, You are faithful to remember
All who call upon Your holy Name.
Therefore, please lead us to the path of salvation
And let us drink of the waters of life everlasting.
Redeem us from death, both man and beast,
And deliver us from the hands of the wicked.
For love never fails and hope in You never dies.
Consider the lowly, the humble, the sad, the meek;
redeem the innocent, the helpless, and the faithful.
And keep all the simple from harm and corruption,
Those into whom You have breathed life.
Forgive us all our dreadful and grievous sins
Both intentional and even unintended;
And let us who have kept the faith join You
In Your glorious kingdom at the end our days.
In the name of God the Father, God the Son,
Jesus Christ, and God the Holy Spirit. Amen.

Special Prayer For The Animals

King of Kings and Lord of Lords,
Remember the lion whose majesty is beheld;
And the regal tiger who reigns supreme in his land,
And the cougar, panther, jaguar, leopard, lynx, ocelot
And other wild cats to whom you have entrusted might.
Let them rule with righteousness and live with dignity.
Keep them from the sin of treating the weak cruelly,
Give them victory without causing unjust suffering.
Protect them from their enemies within and without.
And reveal Your glory to the world through them.
Hunter of Hunters, Maker of the wild,
Be with your bears as they forage for food,
Keep them from disobedience and destructiveness.
Provide for their increasing needs
As man occupies more of their natural habitat.
Let your pandas multiply among the forests
With bamboo to feed them in plentiful supply.
And the koalas that tenderly cling to the trees
Let them dwell in peace and praise.
Almighty Father of all living creatures,
As the deer pants for the water,
So too let the antelope pant after Thee.
So that the moose, deer, wildebeest, caribou
And all of his harmless, graceful cousins
Be permitted to enjoy the splendor of their lives
And feel Your presence in safety and love.
That he not be hunted for sport by man or beast.
That You will guide them through all terrains.
Great Diver of the Deepest Waters,
Who did set the ocean floors in place,

Until We Meet Again

Remember your magnificent sea creatures,
From the very large to the very small.
Be with your great whales as they navigate the oceans
And as they avert the many dangers found at sea.
Use them as messengers as You did with Jonah,
And let them manifest Your awesome grandeur.
Take care of the playful seals
Who can barely protect themselves from hunters,
For they love and nourish their innocent young
And show forth Your humor and community.
For the dolphins, manatees, and other marine mammals
For the colorful fish and other fascinating sea creatures
Let them bring wonder to the world of man
And for so doing, protect them from all harm.
Ancient of Days, Eternal Patriarch,
Remember the elephants Your gentle giants
For they have much love and wisdom
And are often captured and treated unfairly.
And are used for entertainment, resources, and folly
Keep them from those whose hearts are full of evil.
Do not let them be pushed into sin,
But forgive each and every one who is so provoked.
Good Shepherd, Whose sheep know His voice,
Tend each and every lamb,
Watch over them for they are very helpless;
Forgive the rams who push and shove with their horns
Teach them to be noble and to share with their weak.
Let all of the goats follow you and forsake their rebellion
And have abundant mercy upon the cattle
Who are treated so harshly and suffer so very much.
Please save all of the bulls
From those who hate their robust manhood
And make a sport of their destruction before men.
Let them all be saved and delivered from a wretched life.

God's Eternal Plan For His Animals

And for the wild boar or lowly swine,
Who are despised for being dirty and unattractive,
You alone, Oh Cleanser of body and soul,
Can make these animals clean, I pray You do so.
For the apes and monkeys whose faces mock man's
And lead him to the deception of a common ancestry,
Let them rejoice in You and be exceedingly glad,
That You used them to test and prove the hearts of man.
Let them swing from the tree of life set in the garden
And forever sing praises to Your holy Name.
Let it be that the serpent will have learned his lesson,
And that someday he too shall be restored to walk.
For all of the other animals, birds, insects, sea creatures
Far too numerous in type to mention,
Let them all be redeemed for the kingdom
Where there will no longer be any killing or hunting
And there will be no more death and disease.
For all the animals have suffered under the yoke of sin
And their souls groan for deliverance from evil.
Oh Lord, my God and Redeemer,
I have looked into the faces of these animals
And I have seen much love.
They are indeed endowed with the capacity for love
And You promised that love never fails.
So therefore, on behalf of all the animals,
I beseech You for the eternal salvation
Of all those that have walked with love, faith, and hope
And have endured the hardships of this world.
Let them all see the light of life
And find a place in Your holy, luminous kingdom
And be part of your great redeemed family
From all the families of earth.
In the glorious Name of Christ our Savior,
Amen.

Prayer For Special People

Almighty God and Father,
Without You we can do nothing.
But with You we can do anything.
Help those people who are called to serve animals
And care for their basic needs.
This is a burdensome calling for many
And they greatly need your support and compassion.
Those who give a lot also require a lot
Yet too often they ask for so little.
Be their portion and provide abundantly for their needs
So that they may continue in their noble pursuits.
Help those whom You have called to defend
The helpless animals who arrive in harm's way
To win victory after victory, rescue after rescue,
For the sake of Your animal children whom you love.
Save the soul of every loving, dedicated animal worker
That not even one will be lost and eternally separated
From the animals he has loved in word and deed.
Jesus, I pray, that every person who loves Your creatures
Will find salvation by the shedding of Your blood
When you took the role of the lamb of God
Who takes away the sins of the world
For all those who will believe in You.
Stop the injustice and cruelty of the wicked
Who abuse animals for money, power, entertainment
And other evil pursuits.
Let them repent of their deeds and turn around
Or let the punishment for their acts be heavily upon them
And set it as an example to frighten other such cowards.
In the Mighty Name of Christ our Lord,
Amen.

Prayer For Salvation Of The Soul

God My Father, King of my heart,
I know and believe that You sent Jesus Christ,
God The Son, Your only begotten Son, my Savior,
To pay for the price of my wrongdoings,
A penalty that would have required my life.
Your Word says that all transgression leads to death
Because it ultimately leads to separation from You,
For You are holy and cannot be joined to sin.
Though I may not understand everything
About the divine mystery of the cross,
I accept the substitutionary death of the Messiah
In place of the judgment due me.
I am very grateful for this provision,
For without it, I would never be able to live forever
And spend my eternity in Your resplendent kingdom.
Yet You made a way for me to receive this inheritance
And it is apart from the will of man
And the interpretation of man
And the intervention of man.
It is by the supernatural will of God that I am saved
By faith in Jesus Christ, the Word made flesh,
And by obedience to Your commands.
I know that I am not perfect, no ever will be,
And that I will make mistakes in the future.
But I trust and believe that You will guide me
On the path of righteousness for Your Name's sake
And that You will never leave me nor forsake me
In my efforts to remain in You, You will be with me.
Lord, please write my name in the Book Of Life and
Fill me with the Holy Spirit so I may live for You anew.
In the Redeeming Name of Jesus Christ, Amen.

Blessing Upon All The Earth

Awesome Father God,
Masterful Creator with infinite splendor,
Heaven is Your throne, and Earth is Your footstool;
Behold, they are not far from each other.
We look to the sky and ask for Your gracious blessing
upon all the Earth and its inhabitants;
That the majestic seas should unfurl
Like the detailed scrolls of a great scribe
Bearing unmistakable truth to every nation
And impassioned direction to every people.
Let the mountains proclaim Your habitat
As they carry our eyes beyond our imaginations,
Piercing the veil of Your mysteries,
Pointing the way to our eternal home.
Please bless all the trees and green plants,
Love them as they have loved us,
Providing us with the oxygen we need to breathe
Like Your Holy Spirit who is likened to the breeze.
How beautiful are all of your precious gems and stones,
Each one so perfectly formed and capable of radiance
While full of secret meaning that is significant of You.
Bless the soil, make it fresh and rich,
That abundant life shall be nurtured from it
As a loving mother feeds her young.
As we look to the Earth let us find work
Let us not cease from our labors
In making our world a better place
From sun to sun and soil to soil.
Grant us peace and harmony for your name's sake;
Keep man from destroying all these that You have made.

115

Blessing Over Food

Lord, God of all creation,
I lament that I have to eat animals for food
I am deeply sorry that sin has brought this about
That Your harmonious design for all the living
Was to dwell in peaceful, loving co-existence
And that Adam and Eve were vegetarians
Until the Devil stole their purity in temptation.
Please purify the food I am about to eat,
And bless the animals who gave their lives
So that I might eat and live
And carry on a life worthy of their sacrifice,
That I might bring honor and glory to Your Name
And advance Your cause of restoration in the world.
Please be merciful to those animals about to die
So that people who dishonor you can live
In the hope that someday they, too, may repent.
Let the animals receive praise at Your gates
And not suffer tragically in life and death.
Please teach me that gratitude is the attitude
For our lives rest so heavily upon Your provisions
A burden that the animals and plants heavily bear.
May the day come when killing and death cease
And the Garden is returned to all the waiting;
When no longer does anyone or anything
Have to die so that another can live,
And that Your perfect sacrifice
Has atoned and reigns for all.
Amen.

A Story Sent In By One Of Our Readers:

My Beloved, Bambi
By Floyd Jacobs

After losing our rescued Boston Bull Terrier, a precious little dog that had been abused and abandoned before we found him, I felt like I couldn't take in any more dogs because I could never replace my buddy, Bo.

But shortly thereafter, my wife, Margie, found another dog in poor condition at a pet store in Pasadena. She paid six hundred dollars to redeem him.

When she first took him to the car, he jumped in and locked his arms around her neck and clung to her all the way to our office. We also had an English Bulldog, Ruffles, we would take to work every day; and people walking by would look in and smile at him.

Ruffles quickly established territory over his toys and Bambi played with the new ones Margie had bought for him. But it was that evening, when we tossed out a ball for Bambi to chase down, that he got his name. We noticed that he hopped like a deer when he ran, so we named him after one.

One afternoon, my granddaughter was playing around and being particularly noisy. I looked at Bambi and our eyes met in a deep way, as I asked him to go and tell her to quiet down. As soon as I said that, he ran over to her and put his front paws up on her knees and looked straight at her with a serious look. He was trying to tell her what I said. I could see him trying to get the words out. Seeing this, I realized how intelligent my wonderful dog was. He seemed to understand what I said and what I wanted him to do. And I think he even knew a lot more than that.

During the summer, around 4pm, I'd take him swimming next door and toss him a branch to retrieve. If I'd fall asleep during play, he nudge my arm until I'd wake up to play some more. At 6pm, before dinner, Margie would say to him: "Okay, Bambi, it's sing time." Then he would jump up into her lap, raise his head, and howl in a sing-song way. At 7pm, she'd say, "Let's go, boy, it's fight time." Then he'd charge in and jump on the bed and they'd play fight in a furious competition for a few minutes before it was "kiss time" when he'd stop and reach up to lick her cheek.

Bambi had allergies which had to be treated with injections. The first time we took him to the vet for a shot, the doctor said: "I'll have to give him a shot in the hip." Bambi heard and moved to the edge of the table and stuck out his leg for the shot. Seeing this, the vet laughed, and so did we. He never ceased to amaze us.

During the time we had with our beloved boy, he did so many things that let us know just how close he was to us, how much he understood, and how important it was for him to be a pleasing member of our family.

Toward the end of his life, his legs were going, so I couldn't take him on our long walks anymore. I had to carry him on my shoulders, but he was happy just the same, just as long as he was going with me.

His breathing became labored and the vet said it was his heart. Bambi then tried to tell us that his time was growing short. After his last vet visit, he came home and went off to the storage room alone. I frantically ran around searching for him, but when I found him, he had died out of our sight. I believe he didn't want to upset us in seeing him die. I had never felt so lonely and sad, all I could do was cry. But years later, after reading this Book, I now know that I will see Bambi again in heaven.

Papa's Pre-eminent Pets

Does the Father of all creation, have pets of His own? The prophets Isaiah, Ezekiel, and John the Apostle wrote about these mysterious angelic beings who hang around God. These are the Seraphim and Cherubim, and when you read of their descriptions, you will understand why I amusingly also call them, "Daddy's guard dogs."

"... As for the likeness of their faces, they four had the face of a man, and the face of a lion, on the right side; and they four had the face of an ox on the left side; they four also had the face of an eagle." (Ezekiel 1:10)

With those four faces, no one will be getting by them. But what might they look like? Here is another description of similar creatures.

"In the year that king Uzziah died, I saw the Lord sitting upon a throne, high and lifted up, and his train filled the temple. Above it stood the seraphim: each one had six wings; with twain he covered his face, with twain he covered his feet, and with twain he did fly. And one cried unto another, and said, "Holy, holy, holy, is the Lord of hosts; the whole earth is full of his glory." (Isaiah 6:1-3)

That is another amazing eye-witness account of these supernatural creatures who are assigned to preside around God in a way that one might have his own faithful dogs sitting by his side. They were revealed on yet another occasion to St. John which he wrote in his prophecy (Revelation 4:46-8).

"And before the throne there was a sea of glass like unto crystal; and in the midst of the throne, and round about the throne, were four beasts full of eyes before and behind. And the first beast was like a lion, and the second beast like a calf, and the third beast had a face as a man, and the fourth beast was like a flying eagle. And the four beasts had each of them six wings about him; and they were full of eyes within; and they rest not day and night, saying "Holy, holy, holy, Lord God Almighty, which was, and is, and is to come."

These creatures and the role they play are so important to God that He revealed them several times to different servants. And if they reside so closely to Him, they must be extremely beautiful, though words are insufficient to provide an accurate portrait of them. The closest image I can liken them to in my thinking, being described as having eyes all around, would be a male peacock's tail. And since the first part of John's vision of God's heavenly throne says there is *"an emerald bow"* surrounding it, the iridescent blue and green bird reveals more of this mystery than we might expect, even to the crown on his head.

Nature is full of such treasures that speak volumes about their Creator; how wonderful it is to find them, and in so doing, be led to the far reaches of splendor as our delight in Him grows without limit.

May God Fill You With Tender Knowing

Of All The Delights We'll Share When

We Dwell In The Kingdom, Overflowing

And…, Until We Meet Again.

Montford Regis, Inc.

Inspirational Books By Asevimoru

❖ Until We Meet Again:
  God's Eternal Plan For His Animals

❖ Tender Miracles:
  In The Life Of A Christian Sojourner

❖ The Book Of Blessings

❖ Memoir Of A Christian Mystic

❖ The Eight Rings Of Jesus

❖ Sonflowers:
  Prayers From The Valley To The Mountaintop

❖ The Prophet's Prism

❖ God's Green Cathedral
  What Nature Reveals About Its Creator

❖ A Culture Of Angels:
  Being Great By Doing Good

❖ The Positive Principle:
  And Other Mathematical Gospel Delights

The Author has also written a collection of novels
and screenplays, some of which have been produced
as films. For more information: www.seviregis.com

Family Album

Ashley

Cherry

Cherry & Chikky

Sevi & Jesse

Chikky

Sevi & Topaz

Christie & Jesse

Kitty Colony

Jeweliette

Simon

Keva

Sparrow

Tiger & Glory   Glory

Tuskany & Cylkie

Tiffany

Tiger

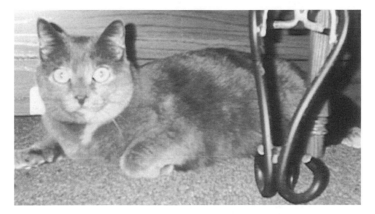

Ginger